For Yoo W9-CRY-460
with my good wishes,
Flo Morse
January 1974

YANKEE COMMUNES
Another American Way

FLO MORSE

Yankee Communes

Another American Way

Harcourt Brace Jovanovich, Inc., New York

Picture Credits

The Bettmann Archive, Inc.: pp. 118, 138; Culver Pictures: p. 133; Hancock Shaker Village: p. 48; LIFE Magazine: photo by John Leongrad, copyright © Time, Inc.–p. 76; The New-York Historical Society: p. 145; Old Economy Village: pp. 85, 106, 110; E. Ray Pearson: pp. 22, 31, 34, 36, 37, 39, 54, 58, 61, 63, 69; Picture Collection, New York Public Library: pp. 28, 29, 57; reprinted by permission of The Plough Publishing Company, "The Shepherd's Pipe," by G. J. Glick and M. Swinger, copyright © 1969 by The Plough Publishing Company: p. 173; The Plough Publishing Company, *Why We Live in Community* by Eberhard Arnold, copyright © 1967 by The Plough Publishing Company: pp. 154, 155, 160, 166, 171, 175; Shaker Museum, Old Chatham, New York: pp. 18, 51.

Curriculum-Related Books are relevant to current interests of young people and to topics in the school curriculum.

First Edition

ISBN 0-15-299710-5

Library of Congress Catalog Card Number: 73-157875

Printed in the United States of America

✛ *For JOE* ✛ ✛ ✛

✝ CONTENTS ✝

Acknowledgments   *viii*

Preface   *5*

   I The Shakers, *Part I:* HANDS TO WORK AND
      HEARTS TO GOD   *13*

  II The Shakers, *Part II:* THE GIFT OF
      COMMUNITY   *45*

 III The Rappites: A HUNDRED YEARS OF
      HARMONY   *83*

  IV The Oneida Community: FAR OUT IN
      THE 1840'S   *115*

   V The Society of Brothers: LOVE AND
      MARRIAGE   *151*

ACKNOWLEDGMENTS

For information—and inspiration—about the Shakers, I am grateful to Sister Mildred Barker and museum director Theodore E. Johnson of the Sabbathday Lake Shaker community in Maine. Professor E. Ray Pearson of the Institute of Design at the Illinois Institute of Technology was generous with his Shaker photographs. These included the detail from a Shaker "spirit" drawing on the back of this book's dust jacket.

Mrs. Lawrence K. Miller was gracious with the resources of Hancock Shaker Village, Pittsfield, Massachusetts, restored by the group she heads, Shaker Community, Inc. Others who were helpful in providing Shaker material include John H. Ott, curator of Hancock Shaker Village, and Robert F. W. Meader, director of the Shaker Museum, Old Chatham, New York.

For new light on the Rappites I am indebted to Daniel B. Reibel, curator of Old Economy Village, Ambridge, Pennsylvania; Hilda Adam Kring of Grove City College; and Dr. Karl J. R. Arndt of Clark University.

A fresh look at the Oneida Community was made possible by two recent books: *Oneida: Utopian Community to Modern Corporation* by Maren Lockwood Carden and *Oneida Community, An Autobiography, 1851-1876*, by Constance Noyes Robertson.

Johann Christoph Arnold has earned my appreciation for his cooperation on the story of the Society of Brothers. And I thank the Rifton, New York, branch of that Society for its hospitality and patience.

Insight into today's communes and alternative life styles has come primarily from *The Modern Utopian*, a magazine edited by Dick Fairfield of the Alternatives Foundation in San Francisco.

My gratitude extends to many others who contributed faith and facts to this book.

Flo Morse

YANKEE COMMUNES
Another American Way

✝ *And the multitude of them that believed together were of one heart and of one soul: neither said any of them that aught of the things which he possessed was his own; but they had all things common. . . . Neither was there any among them that lacked: for as many as were possessors of lands or houses sold them, and brought the prices of the things that were sold, and laid them down at the apostles' feet: and distribution was made unto every man according as he had need.*

—The New Testament, Acts IV: 32-35

PREFACE

A better world is hard to come by, but that's not for want of trying. Over the centuries endless ways have been tried to improve society. One of the most persistent has been communal living. In America a native tradition of separate, "like-minded" communities, following their own way of life, began when the Pilgrims arrived. It blossomed in a golden age of idealistic, utopian communes in the nineteenth century, when the nation was dotted with small, independent communal villages living according to an amazing variety of new social and economic systems.

Some communities were religious, some unreligious. Some were sexually pure or celibate, while others enjoyed free love. Most were communistic, holding all things in common, as the first Christians did. Some gave equal rights to women and freedom to the blacks. Confident of human progress and perfectibility, thousands of Americans left conventional homes, schools, and jobs to live in these would-be samples of a perfect society.

Those times were more pious and more optimistic than ours. But today many people are choosing the same way of group living as a means to social change. Like earlier Americans, they are withdrawing from the world—the troubled Establishment they reject—to set up new miniature, self-sufficient societies. Communal "families" have created farms in the wilderness of the West, Southwest, and New England.

Communal households have sprung up in cities, suburbs, and college towns, where members work and pool their means and share housekeeping and the rent.

To the disenchanted among today's youth, this is a new life style. Many are unaware that living in community is an ancient way of life, that among those who first tried it were a pre-Christian sect called the Essenes and the early Christian church itself, and that America has been Utopia to many before.

Utopia means "nowhere." The word was coined in the sixteenth century by Sir Thomas More—the "man for all seasons"—to describe an ideal imaginary state. Ever since then, those who have conceived or written of a pure or perfect society, too good to be true, have been put down as utopians.

Some utopians, however, did more than dream of better worlds. They put Utopia into practice and demonstrated the good life men could lead. America granted liberty, land, privacy, and unequaled opportunity for some of the most original social and economic experiments of all time. Among the greatest and most enduring were the religious utopias of the Shakers, the Rappites, and the Perfectionists of the Oneida Community. This book introduces those notable forebears of today's communes, and includes the Society of Brothers, a great Yankee commune of the present.

The Society of Brothers—and sisters and children—is part of the Bruderhof ("house of the brothers") movement, which is just fifty years old. Its members were expelled from Nazi Germany in 1937 and forced to flee from country to country, and from the Old World to the New, following the pattern of early communal sects driven by persecution to seek refuge in

America. Just as the communes of the nineteenth century were often visited to see what their way of life was like, so today thousands of people each year inspect the "better alternative" in the three pastoral communes of the Brothers. This interest in the Society shows a new respect for the concept of communal living.

Not long ago the old Yankee communes seemed to be oddities of the past. The later ones were ignored. But now this neglect and inattention are being corrected, as brotherhood—no less than rugged individualism—is recognized as having played a contributing role throughout American history. To those who struggle for a new life in communes today the successful communitarians of the past are logical heroes and heroines. Some who suffer persecution now may be encouraged to learn that although early American mobs beat up Shaker foundress Mother Ann Lee in 1781, the Shakers survived for 200 years.

It is unlikely that any communes of the 1970's will last that long. The world in which new groups gather is itself less durable than it was in the nineteenth century, subject to swifter change and destruction. This makes the communes of today less secure, less committed to lifelong goals, and more impatient. They are not devout communities of obedience, as the Shakers, Rappites, and Oneida Perfectionists were, and they lack their uniformity and the strength lent by fanatic faith.

But in fundamental ways today's rural and urban alternatives to a big, impersonal technological society have much in common with the old groups. They, too, seek peace and freedom in brotherly love, the natural life, and hard manual labor. Through common ownership and wider family relations, they try to avoid selfishness and greed.

In this way, the vision and values of the historic communal movement have lent themselves to the "revolution of the children" and to youth's "counterculture." The rash of communes—mostly homesteads of the young—once more scattered across the nation expresses the ideals of the past, as well as dissatisfaction with the present. And so a new set of utopians, unhappy with the world, impatient with gradual change, generally opposed to violence, is dropping out and inventing its own societies.

They attract all sorts of people. Some are religious, worshiping God or nature. Some are happily married, while others want free love. Some prefer one sex only; others are trying group marriage, which the Oneida Community practiced for thirty years in the nineteenth century. Children in communes are raised together, the way the Shakers raised adopted orphans and the Oneida Community reared an "improved" breed of its own children. Some people are trying to bring to life a scientific utopia called *Walden Two*. Some search for utopia in drugs, which others fear as anti-utopia. Many come together for political activity, racial solidarity, or professional interests. Former nuns live together to extend religious service. Most members of communes are antiwar; some are anarchists.

Today thousands of young people and adults have left affluent homes, good schools, and careers to live and work together according to their various ideals in these large, superfamily circles. Instead of being "nowhere," Utopia to them is still "somewhere" in America, a place for experimental communalism and the social education it provides. "Practical schemes and workable plans," said Emerson, "are always preceded by totally impossible dreams and utopian societies."

During the nineteenth century, that independent American philosopher watched his fellow intellectuals rush into ideal communities like Brook Farm. "We are all a little wild here with numberless projects of social reform," he wrote to Carlyle in 1840. "Not a reading man but has a draft of a new community in his waistcoat pocket. . . . One man renounces the use of animal food; and another of coin; and another of domestic hired service, and another of the State. . . ." Each planned paradise boldly set out to abolish the evil in man and the social evils he created.

Most of the present alternative societies have less sublime objectives. They do not expect to solve man's overwhelming problems of pollution, overpopulation, and the possibility of nuclear war. Human perfectibility—and even human survival— is no longer assumed, as it was in the nineteenth century. What these new groups reflect is the ever-recurring appearance of the communal spirit in times of change. This revival of Yankee communes in town and country, in tents and tepees, and under geodesic domes of flattened car tops, is part of an old and ongoing movement toward a better world.

Far-fetched as it seems, the residents of Drop City, Colorado, and the roamers of the Hog Farm are sisters and brethren to the few remaining Shakers in New England, holding fast to the faith. The kinship in communal living extends to others: in the Northwest and Canada, to isolated Christian brotherhoods of Hutterites, whose ancient history inspired the first Bruderhof in Germany; and to the sect of Dukhobors, whose more radical members protest by marching in the nude. In Israel several hundred *kibbutzim*, agricultural and industrial communes, flourish in the hills and desert. There are fifty *kibbutzim* in Japan, in addition to hundreds of co-operative villages. France has pioneered in communities of work. All over the Continent and England communal experiments are challenging the status quo, and hippie-type clans are making headlines, TV, and the movies, as in America.

The comeback of the commune is a signal of hope, as people keep on trying to make over the world by good example, instead of taking it over by violent means. Out of such hope and experimentation, some progress or promise of a "workable plan," in Emerson's words, may surprise and save civilization. Great new Yankee utopias may arise, so strong again in our day is the urge to common brotherhood in a better life, in an alternative yet traditional way. This way of life had its own pioneers—sons and daughter of a different American revolution. They include the spirited Shakers, the rich unworldly Rappites, the free-loving Perfectionists, and the members of the Society of Brothers, who today stake their lives on a brighter world to come.

CHAPTER 1

The Shakers

Part 1

HANDS TO WORK AND HEARTS TO GOD

At Manchester, in England,
This blessed fire began,
And like a flame in stubble,
From house to house it ran:
A few at first receiv'd it,
And did their lusts forsake;
And soon their inward power
Brought on a mighty shake.

—"Millennial Praises," 1813

On the ship *Mariah* sailing to America in May, 1774, a small band of nine English emigrants danced and sang. There was such whirling, leaping, trembling, shouting, and rolling on the deck that the captain threatened to throw them overboard. But threats meant nothing to these people. They had been stoned by mobs and flung into jail for disturbing the peace and "profaning the Sabbath" in Manchester, where they came from. This was the way they worshiped. They praised God and felt his power in the strange frenzy that gave them the name of Shakers.

It was in the Manchester prison that their leader, Mother Ann, had received a revelation in a vision. While she was praying in a dark stone cell, she felt the spirit of Christ enter into her. As soon as she was released, she hurried to tell the members of her sect, "Christ dwells within me!"

They could see it in the magnetic new radiance about her. And they marveled that the long-awaited Second Coming of Jesus Christ had happened in a mystical way in the heart of one of their own. Ann Lee had been only a poor ignorant factory girl, whose blue eyes were always seeing visions, before she joined the sect of former Quakers at the age of twenty-two. For nine years she prayed and struggled to deliver her soul from sin, suffering great agony of spirit. And now this simple blacksmith's daughter had become the instrument of God. They whom the English mocked as the "Shaking Quakers" were witnesses to her transformation. To this sect she stood side by side with Jesus, not to be worshiped but as the female manifestation of the spirit of God on earth. Their former leaders, Quaker tailors named James and Jane Wardley, who now stood aside, had led them to expect the Second Coming in the form of a woman. In this they had been influenced by the Camisards, French Protestants who early in the eighteenth century had fled to England for the religious liberty to announce their prophecies and issue their strange warnings.

To the common people of Manchester, however, and of course, to the established Anglican church, all of this was blasphemy, traditionally punished by having a hole burned through the tongue with a red-hot iron. But, brought to trial by church authorities, Mother Ann was spared that fate when she cried out in seventy-two distinct languages. The four ministers who were her judges knew she was unschooled and could not even read or write English. Just in case it was a gift of God, they let her go.

Then the mob took matters into its own hands. If she was not a blasphemer, she was a witch, the angry people decided, and began to pelt her with stones. Curiously, she was untouched, and they backed away as they recognized her supernatural protection, and took to fighting among themselves. Another time it was human aid—an unknown nobleman mysteriously arriving on horseback—that saved her from a threatening mob.

Not long after, when the persecution just as miraculously paused, Mother Ann told the Shakers that those with a "gift" or mind to do so should accompany her to America. "I know God has a chosen people in America," she said. "I saw some of them in a vision and when I meet with them, I will know them."

There was only one member of the little group of Believers in Christ's Second Appearing who had substantial means, and he provided the passage money. And the mission was on its way to carry the good news to the colonies and to establish the Millennial Church in America.

On board the ship with Mother Ann were her elderly benefactor, John Hocknell; her brother, William Lee, a tall handsome blacksmith and former horseman in the royal bodyguard; her niece, Nancy Lee; and a pious young weaver, James Whittaker. The others included Mother Ann's rejected husband, the blacksmith Abraham Stanley. He tagged along hoping Ann would change her mind, but she had already persuaded the Shakers to give up marriage as she had given up hers. To Ann Lee sex was sinful, the root of all trouble, and she thought herself punished for her own sexual experience by the early deaths of all four of her children. And certainly now no personal ties could be allowed to distract the Shakers from their special calling to the service of God.

Their devotion took no rest at sea. When they came up from below loudly singing, dancing, and praying, the nine seemed more like ninety to the captain and his crew. The sailors, tired of being lectured on their wickedness, were ready to throw the Shakers overboard, when suddenly a storm sprang up and all hands were needed on deck. The old sailing vessel began to leak. Even with everyone manning the pumps, the sea poured in so fast the captain feared the ship would sink and all would perish. Mother Ann had faith in God and told him not to worry. "Be of good cheer!" she said. "I see two bright angels standing by the mast, and everything will be all right."

Just as she spoke, a great wave towered over them and struck with violent force. Luckily, it slapped loose timbers into place, which stopped the leak and saved the boat. The Shakers got the credit and the captain gladly carried his peculiar passengers the rest of the three-month voyage to New York.

It was August 6, 1774, one year before the Revolutionary War began, when Mother Ann and her eight followers landed in a strange land and trudged over cobblestoned paths from the New York harbor to Queen Street. They stopped in front of the house of a family named Cunningham, and Mother Ann stepped forward and knocked. When Mrs. Cunningham answered the door, she saw a sturdy woman in her thirties in a long Quaker gray dress with a white kerchief pinned modestly across the top of it. The woman's face was radiant and beautiful in her deep bonnet. The American housewife glanced across the road at two other women with men in strange broad-brimmed hats and long-tailed coats over knee-buckled breeches, then back at Mother Ann, who said, "I have come to preach the gospel to America. An angel of God commanded me to make your house my home." Mrs. Cunningham, so the legend goes, had never seen or heard of the people called Shakers, but she took them in.

Here the wonders ceased. Mother Ann worked for the Cunninghams and others as a laundress. Her husband followed his trade until he became ill and Mother Ann was forced to give up her job to nurse him. They almost starved, but once he was better he left her for a woman of the streets, because Ann still denied him the pleasures of marriage.

The rest of the Shakers had ventured north and were trying to clear a tract of woodland that John Hocknell had leased "in perpetuity" from a Dutch landholder. The old man went back to England for his wife, whose family had earlier had him declared insane for joining the Shakers. But now she returned with him to New York, where they found Mother Ann living in poverty. They brought her up the Hudson River to Niskayuna, the Shakers' first communal home in America, eight miles from Albany.

The year was 1776, and all around there was more and more hostility toward Englishmen. But the Shakers hardly realized it. They had no interest in politics, and like the less emotional Quakers they sprang from, they were opposed to war. They minded their own business, struggling to drain and farm their low swampy land and to build a few log houses.

"Put your hands to work and give your hearts to God," Mother Ann told them. It was her most famous and enduring advice.

TESTIMONIES

OF THE

LIFE, CHARACTER, REVELATIONS AND DOCTRINES

OF

OUR EVER BLESSED MOTHER

ANN LEE,

AND THE ELDERS WITH HER;

THROUGH WHOM THE WORD OF ETERNAL LIFE
WAS OPENED IN THIS DAY OF

CHRIST's SECOND APPEARING:

COLLECTED FROM LIVING WITNESSES,

BY ORDER OF THE MINISTRY,
IN UNION WITH THE CHURCH.

The Lord hath created a new thing in the earth,
A woman shall compass a man. *JEREMIAH.*

HANCOCK:

PRINTED BY J. TALLCOTT & J. DEMING, JUNRS.

—◦◆◦—

1816.

At the end of each long hard day they still found the energy to worship with the dancing and the shaking they believed rid them of sin and brought them close to God. The time had not yet arrived to spread the word that the Millennium, a thousand years of heaven on earth, had begun. "Wait," said Mother Ann. "They will come like doves."

Patiently the little English group lived in the wilderness at Niskayuna through the signing of the Declaration of Independence and three-and-a-half years of war. They did not attract much attention until the end of a great religious revival at nearby New Lebanon, New York. The revival had attracted hundreds of people from the surrounding border towns of New York and Massachusetts. Such outbursts of religious enthusiasm were common in the colonies, which had experienced a great awakening during the 1730's and 1740's. It was now the middle of the Revolutionary War, and even though only a small number of Americans were actually fighting, wartime brought men to the brink of eternity. Since the established churches offered no comfort or assurance of salvation, anxious men and women in fear of judgment day and damnation for their sins crowded into camp meetings, held in a big barn. They prayed and repented, wept and trembled, fell into trances, saw visions, and finally danced for joy when the revival preachers promised the end of war and sin and the Second Coming of the Lord.

Title page of the so-called "Secret Book of the Elders." The book consisted of a collection of testimonies in defense of Mother Ann, who at one time had been accused of witchcraft, drunkenness, and prostitution. The "Secret Book" was used solely by Shaker elders.

But after the winter nothing came of all the promises, and the hopes and visions faded. Then among the colonists there was talk of a band of holy strangers living together near Albany. It was said they served God day and night and never sinned.

Single seekers and groups—the serious and the curious— went to Niskayuna to see the people called Shakers, who seemed to be expecting them. The visitors stayed for days or weeks, enchanted by Mother Ann and her joyful, melodious songs, her mind reading and body healing and other marvelous gifts. She comforted them by telling them Christ would come again and again in the hearts of the purest people, who confessed their sins, gave up their marriage beds, and righted the wrongs they had committed. One after another, and singly in private interviews rather than in mass conversions, the Americans welcomed the brand-new faith. Husbands and wives often joined at the same time, and sometimes with their whole families.

The original Shakers, who numbered only about a dozen, were kept busy dancing, counseling, cooking, and keeping a clean house for the crowds that came to their door. They were glad to give up their beds and sleep on the floor, and prayed for their own continued strength and guidance.

Eventually the new Believers went home to found little centers of Shakerism in the towns and villages where they lived in New York and New England. Most of them were plain farmers and laborers, many in their early twenties or younger, but among those first converts was Joseph Meacham, a man of forty and a Baptist minister from New Lebanon, New York, who was a leader of the recent revival. His defection to the

Shakers angered the Baptists, who helped spread rumors that the Shakers were really British spies. Why else were these pacifists separating American families and splitting up engaged couples, they asked? Why were they luring people to join them and bring supplies to their colony?

One day in 1780 a young Shaker driving a flock of sheep to Niskayuna was seized by a mob. The sheep were divided, and the youth was carried off to Albany to be tried for treason. Other Shakers who rushed to his defense landed in jail with him when they, too, refused to swear oaths of allegiance or bear arms. Suspected of witchcraft as well as treason, Mother Ann, with her brother and James Whittaker, was arrested and thrown into jail. She pressed her face against the prison bars and preached to crowds that gathered outside about Christ's new kingdom in America. She even made some converts before she was threatened with deportation and sent down the river to Poughkeepsie to be banished behind the enemy's lines.

Many Americans protested the mistreatment of the Shakers by a country fighting for its own freedom and civil rights. And when it was decided that the Shakers were harmless to the new nation's security, and they were all released, they emerged better known than ever.

The following year, 1781, when the American cause looked darkest, Mother Ann and five elders left Niskayuna to visit the scattered converts and strengthen them in the faith. They were on the road for more than two years and covered thirty-six towns and hamlets in Massachusetts and Connecticut. There they tarried in fellow Shakers' homes and taught all who would listen how to "travel" in the way of God.

Hundreds of Yankees were drawn to their singing-dancing meetings, where confession was heard and the spirit of Christ was whispered to be present in the person of Mother Ann Lee.

The Shaker missionaries' home away from home was near Harvard, Massachusetts, and from there they made side trips to nearby villages. Here Mother Ann confronted the people she claimed to have seen before in the vision telling her to go to America. But there were sinister faces in the picture

The "world's people" watch the Shakers worship.

now, for regularly along their route the Shakers met hostile mobs who threatened their lives for breaking up families and churches. Sometimes, outside the houses where they labored or prayed with new Believers, angry crowds gathered with clubs and whips. They broke in the doors and dragged out the defenseless Shakers by their arms and legs and hair and beat the men for blasphemy until their backs bled. Mother Ann would be ordered to show where the English judges burned a hole in her tongue. "Will you believe your own eyes?" she would ask, pulling off her bonnet and sticking out an unblemished tongue. The men would press forward to see. Ashamed when they saw nothing, they would move back, admitting, "They tell awful lies about you."

The Shakers, who practiced the nonviolence as well as the common ownership of the early Christians, were fearless in facing the mobs. But the injuries and brutality they suffered on the mission to New England shortened their lives. They returned safely to Niskayuna in 1783, just as the Peace of Paris was ending the American Revolution. All of them were battered and scarred, and not long after, Mother Ann's brother William Lee died at the age of forty-four. He who had boldly sung, and even composed hymns, at the moment of persecution proved weaker in body than will; his skull had been fractured.

Nor did Mother Ann ever regain her strength. She had premonitions of her own death and spent her last days trying to comfort her followers and the many pilgrims who traveled to see her and were never turned away. "Don't worry!" she reassured them in her cheerful and inspiring way. "You will see peaceable times, and none of the wicked will make you afraid." Like any mother who knows she has to leave her children, she tried to remember everything that could help them carry on without her: how to manage their households with thrift and raise their families in harmony and how to labor faithfully. In words that lived long after her, she told them, "Do all your work as though you had a thousand years to live and as you would if you knew you must die tomorrow."

She urged them to persevere in the way of God and not to heed the lies circulated about her because she preached against lusts of the flesh. But to the pilgrims she said, "Do not go away and report that we forbid to marry: for unless you are able to take up a full cross, and part with every gratification of the flesh, for the Kingdom of God, I would counsel you, and all such, to take wives in a lawful manner, and cleave to them only; and raise up a lawful posterity, and be perpetual servants to your families: for of all lustful gratifications that is the least sin."

In homely sayings that became Shaker law she counseled against laziness, waste, dirt, disorder, and vanity. Finally she foretold the gathering of her disciples into "a united body, or church, having a common interest." But not in her time. She prophesied that American-born Joseph Meacham, now an elder at the Shaker colony at New Lebanon, would be the one to do the gathering. Her blue eyes peered into the future as she predicted, "The next opening of the gospel will be in the Southwest. It will be at a great distance, and there will be a great work of God."

Just before she died in 1784, a year after her return from the missionary journey, Mother Ann had a vision in which Brother William came in a golden chariot to take her home. And John Hocknell, an old man, but still gifted in visions, insisted that he saw her soul wafted heavenward in just such a chariot, drawn by four white horses. Mother Ann was only forty-eight at her death, but her work on earth was done.

Already the "chosen people in America" far outnumbered the few who had come to the New World to save them. To these American Shakers, Mother Ann was immortal. They did not falter long, and the strong did not "fall away" from the faith when she left them. Her successor was thirty-three-year-old James Whittaker, who as a little boy was said to have kept her alive in an English jail, where she was left to starve, by feeding her milk and wine through a pipe passed through a keyhole.

Father James, an inspired preacher whose zeal was second only to Mother Ann's, began to prepare the Shakers for the next step—separating from the hostile and sinful world. They would have to leave their homes and make a life together for protection and security against persecution. This would mean breaking off natural family ties completely and would be especially hard on young members who joined the sect over the objections of skeptical parents and husbands and wives. Strong leaders would be needed for such a transition, and, seeking them, Father James tried to visit every place Shakers lived, even as far away as Maine and New Hampshire. Some had already set up communal living in the homes of well-to-do members. But those still isolated in their own homes were cautioned by Father James against the world's corruptions. "I warn you, brethren," he said, "not to be overcome with the cares of this world, lest your souls lose the power of God and you become lean and barren." He even disapproved of Shakers in western Massachusetts taking sides on issues like Shays' Rebellion, when poor desperate farmers armed with staves and pitchforks marched against the state.

When he dedicated the first meetinghouse at New Lebanon in 1786, Father James introduced the new "gospel orders" and the kind of discipline the Shakers would eventually live by. "Ye shall come in and go out of this house with reverence and godly fear," he announced. "All men shall come in and go out at the west doors and gates; and all women at the east doors and gates. Men and women shall not intermix in this house or yard, nor sit together; neither shall there be any whispering or talking or laughing or unnecessary going out and in, in times of public worship."

The last of the English Shaker ministers of Christ, Father James wore himself out by his long journeys and his effort to hold the Believers together. Ill health forced him to retire to Enfield, Connecticut, leaving Joseph Meacham in charge of the home church at New Lebanon. And when Father James died in 1787, Father Joseph completed his work of separating the Shakers from the world. As Mother Ann had predicted, it fell to this less saintly and more practical man, their first American leader, to organize the Shakers into a series of independent village-communes, a United Society of Believers in Christ's Second Appearing.

Father James chose a woman, Sister Lucy Wright of Pittsfield, Massachusetts, to be the "leading character in the female line" and set the pattern for a dual order of government with equality of the sexes far in advance of the times. Lucy had been only twenty-seven when, keeping her maiden name, she followed her husband Elizur Goodrich into the Shaker ranks to live as a single woman. Mother Ann was so impressed with her that she called her joining "equal to gaining a nation." Not only was Lucy handsome, forceful, and intelligent, but she came from a good Providence, Rhode Island, family and lent prestige to the Shakers.

Father Joseph and Mother Lucy made their headquarters at New Lebanon, and the New York community became the mother church. It was the first to collect its members into the way of life the Shakers called "society-order." Next to do so was Niskayuna (later called Watervliet), where Mother Ann lay buried in a humble grave. A decade after her death there were ten other Shaker communes in New England, patterned on New Lebanon, at Harvard, Hancock, Tyringham, and Shirley in Massachusetts; Enfield in Connecticut; Canterbury and Enfield in New Hampshire; and Gorham, Alfred, and New Gloucester (later Sabbathday Lake) in Maine.

So many came together in those early years that there were high hopes of saving the world. The challenge rang out:

Hats and broom hang outside brethren's rooms.

"Make room for thousands!" Everyone suffered and sacrificed to expand the kingdom of God for all who wanted to join it. Big communal dwellings were prepared, and the New Hampshire man who framed the first meetinghouse was in great demand. For eight or nine years Brother Moses Johnson traveled from group to group building ten more plain churches without spires—not "the devil's steeple-houses" that Mother Ann had disliked. He also raised barns, hogsties, and gristmills, leaving his stamp on Shaker architecture, before he slid back into the "common course" of the world, not the first or the last of the Shakers to do so.

Bonnets, cloaks, and broom at entrance to sisters' rooms.

Most of the communities grew around estates of stauncher members like Benjamin Whitcher of Canterbury, who had kept a houseful of New Hampshire Shakers for ten years. But it was not only large donations of land and labor that helped establish the new colonies; incoming Shakers made many smaller contributions. As they wound up their affairs, paid off their debts, and withdrew from the world, they brought into the fold all kinds of possessions—livestock and wagons, beds and bedding, grain and feed and household goods. It was not only inspirational, but practical and necessary to follow the example of the first Christians, who "had all things common."

Aiming to be as pure and chaste as they had been, the Shakers separated husbands and wives. Their children were placed in separate orders for girls and boys, where they were no longer the special concern of their parents. They all became part of the extended families that made up each Shaker commune. Every family was governed by a set of elders and eldresses, deacons and deaconesses, and trustees, male and female, who handled the spiritual, social, and business affairs of its thirty- to ninety-odd members.

There were usually three families in a society. New Lebanon at one time included eight families. They were either numbered as they were gathered, or named geographically—Center Family, South Family, Hill Family, and so on.

The central ministry skillfully guided and unified the new way of life, dispatching elders where needed to help the new sisters and brethren adjust and conform. And in the matching societies where men and women were equal and obedient, each sex dressed uniformly and lived at arm's length

Silent meals at separate tables.

from each other. Before long there was "gospel order." This differed from the world's order not only in joint ownership of goods, but in the strict separation of the sexes. Sisters and brethren were forbidden to pass on the stairs, to enter each other's rooms or place of work, to give or receive presents, or ever to touch each other. To safeguard these arrangements and many other social regulations, separate staircases were built wherever possible, separate workshops were maintained, narrow paths and separate doors were used. Also, there were separate dining tables at the common meals eaten in monastic silence.

A daily disciplined round of work and worship honored Mother Ann's major principle of "hands to work and hearts to God." Work was done with care, as Mother Ann had ordered.

The Shakers had begun trades and handcrafts even before the communes were organized, and now their trustees handled sales of garden seeds and medicinal herbs and farm produce to the world. Only trustees dealt with outsiders, who gradually learned to respect the creativity of Shaker hands and to trust the honesty of Shaker hearts. Brethren in broad-brimmed hats went out on the road in America's first one-horse wagons to peddle "things Shaker" to a growing market.

While their occupations were rewarding and profitable, worship was the Shakers' chief joy and recreation. Now that they lived in groups, their dancing meetings were family-style. When Mother Ann had passed like an inspiration among them, they had danced individually to her cry, "Be joyful, brethren and sisters! Be joyful! Joy away! Rejoice in the God of your salvation!" Now there were no more impulsive whirlings, no wandering off alone in a trance, as in her day, after one's own outstretched arm. Instead, everyone memorized the sacred shuffling steps revealed to Father Joseph in a vision of the angels marching and countermarching and circling the throne of God. Not a dancing man, but an intensely spiritual and conscientious one, he practiced the steps alone in his room before teaching them to the Believers.

From Mother Lucy the dancers learned to hold their hands aloft cupped in the ancient prayerful way to receive God's love, and to shake their hands down to release evil. Dancing, rehearsed and structured, with the brethren lined up on one side and the sisters on the other, became an impressive ritual, like Shaker life itself. Later, it became an exhibition, sometimes with 300 or 400 Shakers participating and the "world's people" watching from the sidelines.

When the disciples of Mother Ann were safely within tidy well-run collectives, Father Joseph died suddenly in 1796, exhausted from constant travel and effort. His great work of organization was done: all Shakers had left the world, renounced the flesh, confessed their sins and contributed their property to the church. A simple verbal covenant, all that had bound them until a year before his death, had been put into writing. The way of life "wherein they were called to travel" was making spiritual and practical progress when, for the first time in years, there came an outside diversion.

Mother Lucy was supreme head of the ministry when news reached New Lebanon of a strong religious awakening on the distant frontiers of Ohio, Kentucky, and Tennessee. She was reminded at once of Mother Ann's prophecy and decided to "open the gospel in the Southwest," where the great Kentucky Revival was already in its fifth year.

It had erupted out of a series of camp meetings sponsored by the Presbyterians to stimulate religion on the frontier. But instead of benefiting the established churches, new sects had sprung up. They dispensed with clergymen and creeds and offered revelations and salvation direct from God. The Shakers, who had developed into a full-fledged sect after the New Lebanon Revival, now saw a chance to harvest western souls and grew excited at the possibility of sending missionaries to the frontier.

Early on New Year's Day, 1805, three men from the New Lebanon Community, their baggage loaded on a single horse, set out on foot on a 1,200-mile trip over wilderness trails to Kentucky. Issachar Bates was a Revolutionary War veteran who had fathered eleven children before he joined the Shakers.

Kitchen sisters share their work. "See that your victuals are prepared in good order and on time, so that when the brethren return from their labors in the fields they can bless you and eat their food with thankfulness."

John Meacham was Father Joseph's son. And Benjamin Seth Youngs was a Shaker scholar. They would make good missionaries.

Their path across the country led through New York, Philadelphia, Baltimore, Washington, and then over the Appalachian Mountains. Two months and twenty-two days after they left home they found the "first rest for the soles of their feet" in a simple log cabin in Turtle Creek, Ohio. There, a frontiersman named Malcolm Worley and his wife listened eagerly as the Shakers warmed themselves before the fire. The midwesterners were excited to hear about the new communal way of life and religion. That very night they accepted the faith and confessed their sins to these dynamic men of God, so filled with hope and courage. "All that I have is yours!" promised Malcolm Worley, gripping the hands of the three men. His property became the first Shaker communal holding in the West. Within a few weeks more families joined their small group and added their land and goods.

The most important convert was the Worleys' pastor, Richard McNemar, an educated Presbyterian minister of a reformed or New Light Church. He had been one of the founders of the Kentucky Revival movement, but was forced to watch it grow out of control like a prairie fire and go to extremes.

He told the Shakers how the God-driven people, massed together in the forest, turned from sin to the Lord. Inflamed night and day by the holy spirit, hungry for righteousness and sinlessness, many responded hysterically, screaming in their anguish, barking like dogs, jerking without stopping, baying on all fours, rolling like logs, falling down stiff as corpses.

Community at South Union, Kentucky. A black family of ex-slaves was part of the Shaker community at South Union after the Civil War. Black Shakers lived with white members in many northern societies.

Nonetheless, this enthusiastic revival atmosphere favored the work of the Shaker missionaries. With the minister on their side, and with preaching and singing, they won his entire flock and competed successfully with the old churches and the new sects for the saved. "Here was a people waiting for us," wrote Issachar Bates from the West. "They were very swift to hear and confess their sins, and we left them rejoicing." New Shaker societies were born, and Brother Issachar walked all the way back to New Lebanon for money to buy land to settle them on. In fact, in ten years' time he traveled 38,000 miles, mostly on foot, and listened to the private con-

fessions of more than a thousand new Believers in Christ's Second Appearing.

Among the eastern Shakers, the excitement in the Southwest gave rise to a sympathetic revival and a boost to the faith. Sisters and brethren followed Brother Issachar back to help organize communal homes for "Mother's children" in the West, at South Union and Pleasant Hill in Kentucky, and Union Village and Watervliet in Ohio. Later "there was a gift," as the Shakers put it, to establish colonies at Whitewater, Ohio, and North Union (Shaker Heights) near Cleveland. The westernmost colony, founded at Busro, Indiana, suffered continually from malaria, Indian raids, and the brutal occupation of soldiers, and its members had to move in wagons and flatboats to join the other groups.

Indians were the least of the western Shakers' problems. All the religious prejudice, persecution, and violence of New England were repeated, with the added lawlessness of the frontier mob. Issachar Bates recorded on his journey to Indiana in 1808:

> . . . They came upon us on horseback with ropes to
> bind us, headed by one John Thompson. He stepped up
> to me and said "Come prepare yourselves to move."
> "Move where," says I. "Out of this country," said
> he, "for you have ruined a fine neighborhood, and now
> we intend to fix you. Your hats are too big, we shall
> have a part of them off, and your coats are too long,
> we shall have a part of them off. And seeing you will
> have nothing to do with women, we will fix you so that
> you will not be able to perform. . . ."

Fortunately, the Governor of the Indiana Territory intervened and saved them.

As time passed, the Believers in the West, as in the East, were accepted as good farmers and neighbors. Legend has it that one town in Ohio declined as a result of persecuting the Shakers and another prospered because its citizens treated them kindly. Slowly the western settlements grew in land holdings and became strong in leadership and influence. They all shared in a social system that segregated the sexes while it united the labor of their hands and hearts.

Before the middle of the nineteenth century there were eighteen sturdy Shaker societies, subdivided into fifty-eight family units. On vast and rolling farms, spreading from Maine almost to the Mississippi, 6,000 thrifty Shakers worked toward perfection. They were certain God's kingdom had come and they were living in it, unmarried, and unsullied as angels. They were also proud of the religious communism adopted in their withdrawal from the world. They were the first Yankee —native-born—communists, having inherited the religion and

Intercommunity visits were rare in winter, but Shakers enjoyed their sleigh rides.

way of life followed by one of the earliest immigrant communal sects.

By this time the Shakers—the United Society of Believers in Christ's Second Appearing—offered the best model of the good life possible in small, planned communities. The system of sexual and social equality that was part of their religion was studied and envied by other less successful reformers. By the 1840's there were many nonreligious community hopefuls, as there had been in the 1820's with the inspiration and example of Robert Owen at New Harmony in Indiana. Among them were the New England transcendentalists' Brook Farm, where Nathaniel Hawthorne and an intellectual company milked cows and shared farm chores. Later he wrote satirically about that utopian community in *The Blithedale Romance*. Fruitlands was a short-lived dream of Louisa May Alcott's father, Bronson Alcott, who refused to let his vegetarian communal family even use animals for field work because he considered it slave labor. There was also a legion of phalanxes, profit-sharing associations based on agriculture and industry and a system of labor "groups" and "series." In the farming series were plowing groups, haying groups, planting groups, and milking groups, and in the industrial series, carpenters' groups, shoemakers' groups, and so on. The least attractive work earned the highest wage of ten cents an hour, in these popular American attempts to achieve the fantastic reorganization of society proposed by an eccentric French socialist writer, Charles Fourier.

Even if the more practical Shakerdom was not everyone's idea of utopia, it had become a national curiosity before mid-century. The sober hard-working society that nonetheless danced in its churches won a lot of attention from the general public to whom it had made familiar the idea of people living communally.

During the American Revolution Mother Ann had told her children, "Wait, they will come like doves." And looking for closer and more reassuring religious experience, pilgrims had found their way to the people called Shakers.

The United Society always had high hopes of conversions. On the Sabbath they opened wide the special entrances in the meetinghouses for the "world's people," and inside they set up bleachers. Americans and foreign tourists flocked to the spectacle of the sisters and brethren shuffling and shaking away their sin.

CHAPTER II

The Shakers

Part II

THE GIFT OF COMMUNITY

'Tis the gift to be simple, 'tis the gift to be free,
'Tis the gift to come down where we ought to be.
And when we find ourselves in the place just right,
'Twill be in the valley of love and delight.
When true simplicity is gain'd,
To bow and to bend we shan't be ashamed,
To turn, turn will be our delight
Till by turning, turning, we come round right.

—"Simple Gifts," *revival song, received by inspiration*

In 1843 a celebrated visitor from abroad journeyed to New Lebanon, New York, headquarters of the Shaker church. As he approached the quiet village, he passed a crew of Shakers working on the road and thought them "very wooden men as if they had been so many figure-heads of ships." His carriage continued to the beginning of the village, and at the door of a building where the Shakers sold their wares, he requested permission to see the Shaker worship.

Of all people, Charles Dickens, concluding his American tour, was turned away. He took revenge in his book *American Notes*, in which he described his short visit to the Shakers: "We walked into a grim room, where several grim hats were hanging on grim pegs, and the time was grimly told by a grim clock which uttered every tick with a kind of struggle, as if it broke the grim silence reluctantly and under protest. Ranged against the wall were six or eight stiff high-backed chairs and they partook so strongly of the general grimness, that one would much rather have sat on the floor than incurred the smallest obligation to any of them.

"Presently there stalked into this apartment a grim old Shaker, with eyes as hard and dull and cold as the great round buttons on his coat and waistcoat: a kind of calm goblin. Being informed of our desire, he produced a newspaper wherein the body of elders, whereof he was a member, had advertised but a few days before that in consquence of certain unseemly interruptions which their worship had received from strangers, their chapel was closed to the public for the space of one year."

No exceptions could be made. Whereupon Dickens left and later wrote from hearsay all the unpleasant things about the Shakers he could remember.

The elder meant no offense. The Shakers were entirely occupied with a mysterious influence that had invaded their domain. The "world's people" could not be expected to understand it.

This influence began one day in 1837 when several teen-age sisters at Watervliet, New York, suddenly began to tremble and felt compelled to whirl around their classroom without stopping until they fell into a faint. After they came to, they had greetings from the "spirit land" and tales of a heavenly trip. Other children were affected, and before long adults had seizures, too. The phenomenon traveled from east to west. For the next ten years and longer all the Shaker communes were flooded with spiritual messages, songs and dances seen in visions, inspired drawings, prophecies, and even new book-length revelations of God's will. It was a new high in spirit power, even for the Shakers, to whom spiritualism was nothing new. Their whole history was remarkable. The faith had begun with a vision in an English jail and reached America with the help of two angels at sea. Unusual powers had marked the missionary work of foundress Mother Ann Lee and her few followers. Their strange wordless songs and dancing seemed part of an abundance of supernatural gifts and godsends.

And now among those who never knew her, there had come this remarkable increase in inspiration, which the central ministry solemnly declared to be "Mother Ann's work." And with it the four leading elders and eldresses saw a chance to purge the church of a certain worldliness and vanity that had crept in with material success. They told the Shakers in all the communes that Mother Ann wanted her children to return to the purity and plainness of her time.

And lo! there came divine commands for cleaning house and confessing sin and holding mysterious ceremonies on sacred grounds. At night the Shakers were roused for prayer and marched through their buildings with imaginary spiritual brooms. By day they swept the floors with the actual flat broom they had invented. They scrubbed the brethren's, sisters' and children's workshops with sand, cleared every barn, pen, and field of litter and rubbish, until the communes renowned in America for their neatness were tidier than ever before.

As they labored for the gift to be simple, the Shakers played childlike games. They threw themselves into fantasy and dramatics, and were anything but "grim." "Only a Dickens," someone said, "could describe their antics."

Dickens would have delighted in what went on behind closed doors. But large white wooden crosses kept the public away. The world's people were not thought to be ready for psychic phenomena and would only ridicule or fear it. Meanwhile, business continued as usual during the spiritual alterations—dealings in packaged seeds and herbs, brushes and brooms, chairs and oval wooden boxes, sold with the Shakers' famous trademark of honesty and good measure.

Sacred Shaker dance at a secret mountain meeting.

Who had time for the courteous reception of outsiders, when the great of all ages were dropping in? Noah, Alexander, Napoleon and his generals, Queen Esther and George Washington, to name a few, were visualized by the Shakers, to whom the departed were as real an influence as the living.

Even Jesus was reported to be dwelling among the Shakers in this period. In 1843, while thousands of followers of the Reverend William Miller, who predicted the end of the world, waited on roofs and mountain tops for the Second Coming, Shakers in Ohio complacently claimed Jesus was with them at North Union. When the world did not end as expected, some of the disappointed Millerites went insane, and some committed suicide. Some went home and picked up their old lives. Many joined the Shakers, who believed the Millennium had already arrived.

These newcomers, and others from communal sects that foundered, were always welcomed by the Believers. And welcome, too, during this revival, were the wandering spirits of pagans—Africans, Orientals, Indians, and Eskimos—who came seeking salvation. That the dead could still be converted to find eternal rest in heaven was a belief of the Shakers of those times. To them, heaven was a Shaker community on a large scale, where Jesus and Mother Ann were head elder and eldress. Both the Son and the Daughter of God kept in close touch with Shakerdom, the eighteen heavenly societies below. At this time Mother Ann sent frequent messages through members who were called mediums or instruments. Once at a meeting in Watervliet, New York, a sister whirled around in one place for fifteen minutes without stopping or becoming dizzy. Then she ran and whispered her message to the eldress, who gave her permission to announce, "A tribe of savage Indians has been around two days. They're outside the building now, looking in the windows! Mother Ann says to take in the poor spirits and assist them to get salvation!"

Only a new convert might look fearfully toward the windows. But the others entered into the game. The doors were thrown open, and the sister who could "see" the Indians invited them to come in. At once the Shakers became "possessed" of the spirits of squaws and braves. They squatted on the floor together in Indian style, while the elders and eldresses tried to keep them apart in Shaker style. A regular powwow took place, with whooping and yelling and singsong, before the Indians were considered saved and the sisters and brethren returned to their normally dignified selves.

Many Shakers had to labor for "the eye of faith" in order to share the "visitations" and spiritual fun and see the presents Mother Ann sent her children—samples of what waited in God's country for a faithful Shaker who denied his flesh on earth. There was heavenly wine from her celestial vineyard, which made the Believers drunk; glorious crowns and robes they dressed up in; caskets of treasure they divided; baskets of fruit they devoured; and musical instruments they tooted and plucked as they marched around in a parade. A special shipment of spiritual guns arrived for the brethren from George Washington.

Under the influence of spirits, the Shakers sang, "Come, come, who will be a fool?"—and each in an effort to be humble would answer, "*I* will be a fool!" They shared the laughing gift, lodged by a spirit in a medium without a sense of humor. Fortunately, the gift was contagious and traveled around at a

After whirling like a top, a **Shaker** medium falls into a faint.

meeting until everyone rocked in his straight-backed chair, or even rolled on the floor.

Excitement simmered beneath the outward calm of each Shaker communal village. No one knew who would become an instrument next, seized by the spirit and personality of someone who had departed from this life. A sister or brother could be struck down to the floor and struggle as if with a demon, or else be set spinning like a top, or rush back and forth as if driven by the wind. Sometimes the mediums fell into a swoon and remained in a trance for hours or even days, while the family tiptoed around them, eager for their first words or notes.

Nothing seen or heard in vision was ever rejected by the democratic Shakers. Each gift of song—no matter if there were thousands—was prized and recorded in the peculiar musical notation given to Mother Ann by inspiration. There was some warning about "overstepping the real gift" and pretending to be God's Holy Anointed One when one was not. Occasionally, false spirits were discovered through the spiritual "spectacles" or insights of the elders, who listened to all messages first and were not beyond using a medium to expose sin.

Most of the inspiration, however, flowed in and out of pure hearts. Sometimes a sensitive person "in the gift" was excused from his or her normal duties to retire to a quiet place, returning with twenty or more songs in a single day. It was a gift in itself for the Shakers to be able to sing some of the songs, since many mediums spoke in unknown tongues, and to dance in authentic native fashion with the pagan spirits.

Moreover, the Believers who were moved to draw or paint their heavenly visions had never been artists before. The Shakers disapproved of pictures and hung none on their walls. They were counted among the vanities of the world, like ornate clocks, looking-glasses and bureaus, and odd or fanciful architecture. Usefulness was the sole criterion in their own built-in cupboards and functional furniture and in their massive family dwellings, shops, and barns. And if in the creation of utility they produced a singular beauty, it was incidental. "Let it be plain and simple," went a Shaker tenet, "of

good and substantial quality, unembellished by any super-
fluities which add nothing to its goodness or durability."

Completely contrary to "Shaker order" were the spirit or
inspirational drawings. They were full of forbidden, worldly,
and probably longed-for ornaments, quaint symbols, and
small cramped verses and blessings in neat spidery script.
Drawn with joyful flourishes, though not abandon, were
wings of freedom, swords of power, trumpets of wisdom,
crowns of glory, doves of love, birds of paradise, tempered by
cups of humility. Colors like red, ordinarily considered im-
modest, were used. But who could refuse a Valentine from a
vanished hand, probably female, because it was delivered in
red ink?

"I received a draft of a beautiful tree," wrote inspired
Sister Hannah Cahoon from the "City of Peace" (Hancock,
Massachusetts), "pencilled on a large sheet of white paper
bearing ripe fruit. I saw it plainly. It looked singular curious
to me. I have since learned that this tree grows in the spirit
land. Afterward, the spirit showed me plainly the branches,
leaves and fruit painted or drawn upon paper. The leaves
were checked or crossed and the same colors. I entreated
Mother Ann to tell me the name of this tree, which she did
Oct. 1st, 4 hour p.m. by moving the hand of a medium to
write twice over, 'Your tree is the tree of life.' "

It was a favorite Shaker symbol. Father James Whittaker
had seen a burning vision of such a tree before he set out
with Mother Ann to establish the Millennial Church in America.

By the mid-1840's the Shakers had given good measure
to a "swift-winged" Holy Angel, who had demanded, "More
zeal, more life, more fervency, more energy, more love, more

thankfulness, more obedience, more strength, more power!"
Within the next few years, they stopped trailing home exhausted from semiannual pilgrimages to the "feast grounds"
that each community had been ordered to set aside and en-
close. On these holy mounts and sacred plains they had sown
spiritual seed, washed in spiritual fountains, and danced in the
early "promiscuous" style, each Shaker for himself. Gradually,
the communities ended most of the rituals required during the
era of Mother's Work and closeted the spiritual brooms.

The Tree of Life in this inspired, or "spirit," drawing is a symbol of
the Shaker church.

Fewer and fewer messages were divinely posted, although inspiration remained a Shaker gift.

Some thoughtful Believers had been put off by what seemed child's play. Others were proud of the imaginative resources unleashed. Among these were two major revelations. One had a mouth-filling title—"A Holy, Sacred and Divine Roll and Book from the Lord God of Heaven to the Inhabitants of Earth"—and 500 copies were proudly dispatched to the rulers of the world. Later it was discredited. The only one who took it seriously enough to say thank you was the King of Sweden and Norway.

The other king-sized manuscript was a Shaker seeress's defense of extrasensory perception and the possibility of God's continuing to express his will. Why not consider God's revelations a growing thing, like natural science, she asked, instead of something delivered once and for all time?

The worst result of the spiritualist revival was the loss of the outstanding member of the western groups. After thirty-four years as a leader, Richard McNemar was expelled from the order when a medium falsely denounced him to a jealous elder. At the age of sixty-nine, he was given only his clothes and his printing press to enable him to earn a living elsewhere. When the ministry in the East learned what had befallen him, McNemar was reinstated. But by that time he had grown ill and soon died.

No wonder Mother Ann was heard by a medium to grumble, "I foresee the evil of my word being too plenty among the people." The spirits who dwelled among the Shakers announced their own departure and went off, according to the Believers, to manifest themselves to the world. The United

Society waited. And sure enough, in 1848, a strange influence began to stir among the "world's people." It started with young girls, just as it had among the Shakers.

Two farmer's daughters in Rochester, New York, began to communicate with a mysterious spirit who rapped on the walls of their house at night. "Here, Mr. Splitfoot," taunted one of the girls, referring to the cloven foot of the devil, "do as I do!" She tapped—and the spirit tapped back.

The Shakers insisted that their spirits had produced the Rochester rappings. They were very much interested in the exchange, which became so famous that the girls performed it before great crowds in public lecture halls. Even though it later turned out that they were just cracking their joints, Katie and Maggie Fox—and not the genuinely inspired Shakers—got the credit for the birth of modern spiritualism in America.

Though the Shakers considered the new American spiritualism theatrical, they themselves were onstage once a week. The Sabbath meetings were reopened to the public, and many people came to see the show. Some spectators even contributed money to the Shakers in return for the entertainment they received.

If the sisters and brethren felt self-conscious in front of an audience of "world's people," it was not for long. Moving from half-circles at each end of the room, the men on one side and the women on the other, with the singers in the middle, they were soon swept up in the joy of the sacrament. Onlookers shared the thrill of the quick-footed worshipers, who danced in a throng in perfect rhythm with symbolic gestures of their hands.

Shakers worship in the dance, hands cupped to receive God's love.

More than anything else, the dance communicated the kind of joy and freedom there was in being a Shaker—freedom from the evils and pressures of the world, freedom from the burden of sins of the flesh. The purity and virginity of which they were so proud were reflected in the sisters' Sunday gowns of white, with white caps, blue aprons and blue pointed, high-heeled shoes, and the brethren's long-tailed blue coats and trousers. Before long the coats were discarded and the men danced in their shirtsleeves—and never touched the women.

A singing meeting brings sisters and brethren face to face.

For this performance there were rehearsals during the week, and new songs and dances were practiced. At evening social meetings, six or eight brethren sat in a row of straight chairs facing a row of sisters four feet away. There was conversation as well as singing, and it was a more congenial grouping than it looked.

Sometimes sitting opposite the brethren were the sisters who took care of their household and wardrobe needs. The women sewed their buttons and made their beds in the morning after the men left the room and all bedding had been hygienically aired. This natural social arrangement was one that caused malicious gossip outside the communes. The virtuous folk who shook themselves free of sinful thoughts were never able to shake off the slander of a deserted husband or wife whose mate had joined them, or the exposés of those who "fell back" into the world. Shaker celibacy, with men and women living on the same floor in the same household, stirred the public's imagination and indignation. Throughout the nineteenth century many detailed accusations and many suggestive descriptions of short stays among the Shakers were read as eagerly as novels.

Gossip also accused women of signing the covenant to lure away one of the brethren for a husband. One sister did run off with no less than a New Hampshire elder. But for the few exceptions there were hundreds more who embraced Shakerism as a refuge from marriage or the need to marry for economic and social security. Long before women's liberation movements, the Shakers guaranteed the rights of women and gave them every opportunity to progress, or travel. A line of notable women reached the position of eldress, where they were completely equal with elders in governing.

The Shakers' material comforts and social advantages were much admired. Some observers thought even a man could do no wiser thing than join them. Many a "winter Shaker" put up with what he privately considered ridiculous ceremonies for a good warm home until spring.

Despite large numbers of transients, freeloaders, and backsliders, the Shaker societies reached peak membership and prosperity in the decade before the Civil War. This was the golden age in the peace-loving hamlets, where paint never peeled from the buildings and the crystal windows reflected heaven. Nothing was "foul or noisy" along the neat avenues, and when the poet Walt Whitman came to visit, even the dust in the road seemed pure to him.

Daily, at specific hours, the inhabitants rose, prayed, ate, labored, held meetings, and retired. No one was overworked, and there was a wide variety of occupations. Shakers took great pleasure in improving their skills and mastering several trades. Everyone worked, including the elders and eldresses in the special ministry shops. It was almost natural that out of such industry—so many "hands to work"—there would be a flow of invention, an outpouring of mechanical gifts.

The list is long of things the Shakers made first or made better: among them, the common clothespin, cut nails, the flat broom, the circular saw, a metal pen, a rotary harrow, a tongue-and-groove machine, a screw propeller, a threshing machine, an improved washing machine, a pea sheller, an apple parer, a revolving oven, and an improved wood-burning stove. They also made water-repellent cloth and combination window sash.

Hundreds of additional time savers, shortcuts, gadgets, and plans for organizing huge building and irrigation projects were traded like songs and recipes among the fifty-eight energetic families in the chain of Shaker societies across the nation. Sometimes an outsider took advantage of their groundwork in research. The vacuum vessel that Gail Borden borrowed and used for several months among the Shakers at New Lebanon led to his profitable invention of condensed milk.

For a long time the Shakers had no trouble keeping down on such creative farms the many young people, or-

Shaker children.

phans, and unwanted children they took in from the world. There were no public institutions for their care. The Shakers' charity was in part self-interest, a source of future members needed for the survival of the faith. Some societies preferred even bad children to none, while others would adopt only those who came with their parents, often widowed mothers seeking a safe haven, or children left with them by a widowed father. Whenever there were national and local epidemics and disasters, the Shakers sent generous amounts of money and wagonfuls of food and clothing to victims, in addition to offering shelter to orphans.

The children were brought up, educated, and taught a trade or useful arts by members who were devoted to them. In the children's order they lived regulated, happy lives, with many companions and dedicated caretakers. Like their older sisters and brethren, they were expected to keep step, follow the lead and march together toward heaven and life eternal. "The Youth's Guide in Zion" instructed: "Never try to run on ahead before the main body of good believers, and above all, never fall back; but keep up close and be in the gift."

But how did one obey the elders and "the gift" at the same time? A boy who lived with the Shakers was asked whether he could do as he pleased.

"Of course," replied the youth, "We can do whatever we have the gift to."

If he wanted to go ice skating on a winter morning, what would he do?

"I would tell the elder that I had a gift to go down and skate."

Would the elder let him go?

"Certainly," said the boy, "unless the elder had a gift that I should not go."

But if he told the elder that he had a gift to go down and skate and he must go . . . ?

"Why, then," said the boy, "the elder would tell me that I had a 'lying gift' and *he* had a gift to beat me if I did not go about my work at once!"

Corporal punishment was actually rare. In its place, Mother Ann's advice for raising children was applied. She did not believe that children inherited "original sin." "Little children," she said, "are nearer the kingdom of Heaven than

Two young Shakers at Canterbury, New Hampshire, where Shaker boys had their own small farm.

those who have grown to riper years. They are simple and innocent, and if they were brought up in simplicity, they would receive good as easily as they would evil." Partial to young people, she warned parents, "Do not speak to children in a passion, or you will put devils into them. Do not cross them unnecessarily, for it makes them ill-natured, and little children do not know how to govern their nature."

As the young Shakers grew older in the company of consecrated workers, they took their place in the households and shops and gardens that were extensions of the church. They learned to do all their work in Mother's way—as if they had a thousand years to live and as they would do it if they were to die the next day. They learned from the seedsmen how to grow and select the garden seeds that Shakers were the first to package and which they had been selling since 1790.

At New Lebanon they built slat-back chairs, rocking chairs, chairs that tilted back on a ball in a socket, and some that even swiveled. They gathered and cultivated wild medicinal herbs and roots—bugle, belladonna, burdock, horehound, sweetfern, wintergreen—for the extracts, salves, and syrups that were Shaker remedies, as well as for use in the medicines made by "the world."

In the tall brick dwellings the girls cleaned the rooms well, having been taught that "good spirits will not live where there is dirt." They hung chairs and garments on the high peg boards that lined every Shaker room, and swept the floor beneath them. In the fragrant kitchen they prepared wholesome food, and in the common dining room none of it was wasted.

Later many of the skilled young farmers, artisans, and

housekeepers marched off—to tunes more exciting than gift songs—to factories and cities. Few of the children raised by the Shakers—only one or two in ten—remained to sign the covenant that gave their lives to God. Countless youths, however, carried away lifetime habits of neatness, thrift, industry, and Shaker traits of brotherly love and kindness. The Shakers failed to replace the young through other conversions. This loss—plus the industrial competition of an age with bigger machines than theirs—pushed the United Society past its prime.

Still, it had the gift to persist for another hundred years.

During the Civil War the Shakers again had to defend the pacifist principle that had been theirs since Mother Ann and her little band stood up to English and American mobs. They had a great spokesman in Elder Frederick William Evans, the best-known and most broad-minded of the later Shaker leaders. He was an English social reformer who emigrated to America in 1820 with his brother. Together they edited radical newspapers calling for land reform, women's rights, and the end of wage slavery. Interested in the utopian communities springing to life, Evans investigated them all. A strong personal mystical experience commended the Shakers, whom he joined in 1830.

Because his gift for leadership was recognized, Evans quickly leaped the ranks to become chief elder at New Lebanon. And from that Olympian post he urged the Shakers out of their traditional isolationist thinking and into the national movement for social reform. Many Believers thought him too worldly—and too conspicuous. He traveled abroad, carried on a wide correspondence with people like Tolstoy and

Henry George, wrote pamphlets on controversial public issues, and contributed articles to the national as well as the Shaker press.

President Lincoln found Evans an exceptionally able man when he went to Washington in 1863 to petition for draft exemption for the Shakers. He pointed out to the President that the Shakers had saved the United States Government more than half a million dollars. Many members who had fought in the Revolutionary War and the War of 1812 before becoming Shakers had never drawn their soldiers' pensions.

"Well," asked Lincoln, "what am I to do?"

"I can't advise the President," Elder Frederick answered.

"You ought to be made to fight," said Lincoln. "We need regiments of just such men as you!" Nevertheless, he granted the petition giving the brethren an indefinite furlough.

Neither warriors nor slaveholders, the western Shakers still suffered the ravages of the Civil War. Their homelands lay in the shifting battlefields of Kentucky and southern Ohio, and their trade was primarily with the South. The commune at South Union, Kentucky, served 50,000 meals to the hungry soldiers of both the Union and Confederate armies, who crowded to their kitchen doors and windows. And they lost $100,000 worth of buildings, livestock, and business, as well, through theft, maurauders, and money in bad debts.

This community had been founded on the site of the Kentucky Revival, which had brought so many souls into Shakerdom. Some of its first members were slaveholders who freed their slaves as soon as they joined the Shakers. Forty ex-slaves became Shakers, too. For many years they lived in a Negro commune with its own elder. From time to time some of them left for greater freedom, but many died in the faith. When the black commune grew too small, the members were taken in among the whites to live in integrated Shaker order. Negroes had been living in some white Northern communities for a long time. And a black family in Philadelphia was the first urban commune, with the sisters going out to work by day for the "world's people."

As much at home among the Shakers as blacks were former Jews, Catholics and Protestants, Adventists—as the Millerites were later called—and even nonbelievers and agnostics. The Shakers were always on the side of freethinkers and doubters, and opposed to rigid systems of religious belief.

Their leaders, or "leading characters," were early defenders of civil rights, constantly seeking tolerance, justice, and free speech for minority groups like themselves. They even defended the notorious Oneida Community in its religious communism of love. On his part, Oneida founder John Humphrey Noyes, in a book on American socialism, called the Shakers "the most influential social architects of modern times." He doubted whether his own or any of the other communities, religious and nonreligious, could ever have existed without their inspiration and example.

The Shakers were frequently called on by dignitaries like Edwin Stanton, Henry Clay—a western favorite—and Andrew Jackson, and commented on by literary visitors like Hawthorne, Melville, Emerson, Cooper, Howells, and Horace Greeley. Newspaper publisher Greeley was a happy patron of the American communal movement, especially the Fourieristic experiments in the phalanxes of the 1840's. In "association," he was confident, "the future may be assured."

Some admirers of Shaker socialism questioned the supernaturalism that remained an integral part of Shaker life. Elder Evans had to explain in a letter to Count Leo Tolstoy, that "spirit intercourse between parties in & out of mortal bodies" belonged primarily to the early church. The important thing for the author of *War and Peace* to realize was that a "poor illiterate, uneducated factory woman has confounded the wisdom of all *men*—reformers, legislators, and scholars, who have come to nothing as promoters of human happiness."

Evans urged him to found a Shaker order in Russia. But first he must come to New Lebanon to see how "we—the Shakers—under the American secular government carry out the . . . principles of the Christ spirit more perfectly than has ever been done by mortal men and women." He added, "Just as we carry out sexual purity, notwithstanding the sexes are brought face to face in everyday life, living without bars, in the same Household of Faith.

"See what God hath wrought!" he boasted. "Seventeen communities of people whose every right is secured to them, whose every rational want is supplied. . . . Our sisterhood are redeemed. The rights of women are theirs, the rights of property we enjoy. Capital and Labor are at peace. Hygiene is religion with us."

But the tall, stooped elder with his deep-set serious eyes had to watch the number of such fortunate people dwindle. Their energies, if not their advantages, decreased even as he spread their name. By now it was hard to maintain Shakerism at home, let alone sell it abroad, where he had tried a second time in England in 1880 at the age of seventy-nine.

Few were embracing the religious life that demanded so

Elder Frederick Evans was well known among the "world's people."

much of its members and kept them secluded in the country. There was more resignation than inspiration in some members' continued seeking of human perfection. With diminished numbers and reduced zeal, six Shaker villages closed between 1875 and 1900, and the surviving members moved to other communes. Some of the vast land holdings—each society had an average of 2,700 acres in 1875—were sold off or entrusted to hired hands. Many home industries were dropped, and the Shakers bought some of the assembly-line products of the world.

Elder Frederick shook his head when the looms stopped weaving Shaker cloth. "We buy more cheaply than we can make," he said, "but our homemade cloth is much better than what we can buy. And now we have to buy three pairs of trousers where before we made one. Thus our little looms would even now be profitable—to say nothing of the independence we secure in working them."

One new trend he favored was the broadening of Shaker life. The Believers began to read the world's newspapers and magazines, and books on science, history, and travel. They held reading meetings and had debating clubs. Purely pleasure-giving flowers and pictures and musical instruments were finally enjoyed. And why not? said Elder Evans. Saints deserved the good things of the world as much as sinners.

To hold the interest of the younger members, family problems were discussed in open meetings. But no one listened when young women wanted out of the kitchen, or yearned to let their hair grow free of the ever-present bonnets and indoor caps, which some in the West pushed back to their ears.

The only change allowed in the sisters' costume was the replacing of the separate shoulder kerchief with a yoke that still hid the bosom.

It was not until many years later that some of the sisters got their wish for less monotony. They had long outnumbered the brethren and were destined to outlast them. As the men grew fewer, the sisters took over more of the support of the families. They escaped from the communal kitchens and took to selling their confections in Shaker booths at country fairs. They became a familiar sight traveling in pairs to New England seaside, lake, and mountain resorts, where they peddled their small well-made wares and fancywork.

While Elder Frederick was busy at church headquarters with public relations, the quality and structure of local leadership elsewhere declined. Too many elders now wore two hats and, as part-time trustees, paid too little attention to spiritual matters. There were great financial losses, not only from uninsured fires and less productive farms, but from careless or foolish speculations and worldly investments, and even a lack of principle on the part of distracted leaders. Trying to hold things together, they neglected the faith and made things worse.

The old ingenuity and enterprise that once put the Shakers ahead of their time was declining. They became obsolete when machines separated man's hand from his work. Shakers could not understand a world that no longer saw work as an end in itself, a satisfying human activity. They could not keep up with such competition. Nor could they compromise. Shakers had "no middle way, no tolerance for halfway work," in Father Joseph's words. Labor was uniquely related to their worship of God, who was in every piece of wood, every garden. The motive was never profit, but the inspiration of the prophetess Mother Ann, the mother of their invention. Unfortunately, her voice was growing distant. There were no more Shakers who could hear it clearly or recall her unusual powers, like old Abijah Worster, the last survivor of the Harvard, Massachusetts, community. He carried to his grave this vivid memory:

"As I was tossing—tumbling—rolling—jumping—throwing myself against the wall—the chimney—the floor—the chairs, in fact everything that did not keep out of the way, I felt that my blood was boiling, and every bone in my body was being torn asunder, my flesh pinched with hot irons, and every hair on my head were stinging reptiles. I had laid me down to die, when Mother Ann came along, saying, 'Why, Abijah, there is some of the worst looking spirits on your shoulder I ever saw in my life.'

"I crawled along and laid me down at her feet and prayed her in mercy to help me; she raised me up and made a few resolute passes from my head to my feet, with her hands, and I was relieved at once,—and I have never doubted since."

Nor were there any left with the drive of Issachar Bates, who at fifty had walked back and forth between New England and Kentucky to found the western Shaker communes, and who later wrote: "My health is not very good, probably in consequence of having to travel seven miles every day to & from my work at the mill, sometimes in mud and water up to my knees, but my faith is everlasting and I mean to keep it."

Although they, too, kept the faith, they lost the fire, those latter-day Shakers following narrow paths through their communities and through life. When they went forth to worship, they were less nimble and spectacular than they had once been. They lost their audience, and by the end of the century they stopped dancing. The worship service moved out of the big empty meetinghouses and into upstairs rooms of the dwellings. Organ music helped the fewer and faded voices in thousands of simple hymns and vision songs they loved to sing.

In the early twentieth century the Shakers were condensed into fewer and fewer societies. Yet of all the nineteenth-century Yankee communes, only they had marched into the twentieth century with their convictions and communism intact. Much of the sturdy graceful furniture was sold, and some of the villages were occupied by institutions, schools, and churches. There, men and boys continued to live in the old communal buildings in the monastic order of which the Shakers approved.

"Do they marry?" Eldress Sarah Collins asked of the agent for a communal group that wanted to buy the South Family property at New Lebanon in the early 1940's. The applicant was a religious community driven out of Nazi Germany and welcomed in England until World War II. Now forced to leave Britain or be interned as enemy aliens, the Bruderhof, or Society of Brothers, wanted to settle in America.

Eldress Sarah thought it would be nice to have a Christian commune in the silent buildings—especially a pacifist one. The first great international peace conference had been sponsored by the Shakers at New Lebanon in 1905, with more than fifty nations represented. The new group, however, must not be the marrying kind.

It was.

"Nay, then it won't do," decided Eldress Sarah. "True communal living cannot be realized on the basis of the private family." She lived on till her nineties, as many Shakers did, and with fingers knotted from decades of chair-making, she built the last Shaker chair in 1947. A boy's school moved into New Lebanon.

The last Shaker brother died at Sabbathday Lake, Maine, in 1961. Fourteen sisters in their forties to nineties survive him there and at Canterbury, New Hampshire. These two communes, formerly considered "the least of Mother's children in the east," linger on in what one of them refuses to call the twilight of the Shaker faith. At Sabbathday Lake they see Shakerism as ongoing, "something that will last because something made it last, and because it is needed."

"The world needs our prayers," says tiny, white-haired Eldress Gertrude Soule at a private Sunday service in Maine. Her blue eyes peer through steel spectacles as she faces the aging sisters sitting on long benches in the spare upstairs chapel.

On the other side of the room from the sisters are a few male visitors and the resident museum director, a near-brother of this Shaker remnant. The only other onlookers are outside the tall shining windows—old maple trees, which the Shakers often planted, stretching across Route 26 out of Grey, off the Maine turnpike.

Sister R. Mildred Barker, a trustee in her seventies, and the family spokeswoman, plays the organ for the opening hymn. Then in her plain dark dress and thin white cap, she takes her official place on a bench behind the eldress, who also wears an indoor cap. The small congregation of sisters needs no further accompaniment. They sing with vigor and know by heart hundreds of the old songs, which they have recorded.

Most of the sisters no longer wear caps, and their hair is worn as they wish it. Their dresses are printed in small bright patterns in the same yoke-front style of seventy-five years ago, shortened a few inches above the ankle. Each sister makes a contribution to the service, a brief reading or a personal comment on self-improvement. Sister Mildred reflects aloud on some words of Mother Ann: "Heaven is a state of mind."

In that state of mind these serene sisters live. Nine older women on 1,900 acres sloping down to Sabbathday Lake, they sell the potato and corn crop, rent out the orchard of 2,000 trees, and freeze their own garden vegetables. During cold Maine winters they make small products to sell to visitors in the summer. They live by the bell in Shaker order, beginning with early morning prayer. They walk through one door of the common dining room, while the museum director goes through another; he and any men visiting sit down at a separate table.

Sister Mildred, who was brought to the Shakers at seven after her father died, receives the world's people in a room furnished with a row of old-fashioned rocking-chairs (none Shaker), one over-stuffed chair and a television set, which was a gift. For the Shakers of today, like those of yesterday, have many callers, correspondents, and friends. Some of her time is spent searching for Shaker furniture at country auctions and buying it back for the buildings that have become a

Sister Mildred Barker of the Sabbathday Lake community in Maine believes that Shakerism will last, because it is needed.

museum. Much of her time goes into the business management of a scholarly magazine called *The Shaker Quarterly*, published since 1961 at Sabbathday Lake.

At Canterbury, New Hampshire, the remaining sisters are older. There, until her recent death, lived Eldress Marguerite Frost, who more readily admitted that the Shakers have had their day—a good long one and a model to many. Of today's young people who seek a better way of life and come to visit the museum at Canterbury, where they have heard one once existed, this white-haired eldress used to say, "We have what they want." Many Millerites in the 1840's, who never got to heaven on either of the days they expected the world to end, found peace among the Shakers at Canterbury. "The Millerites," Eldress Marguerite noted, "made good Shakers." And she hoped that those turning away from the world today will find something with as lasting value as they did.

These fourteen sisters are the last of the Shakers, a special people born when they say the spirit of Christ made its second appearance in the humble person of Ann Lee. They are still trying to pass the word that the kingdom of God is now and that those in whom the true Christ spirit resides can always enter. They want the world's people—eager antique collectors of all things Shaker—to know about the religion and the communal way of life that inspired personal purity as well as manual perfection.

In big solid dwellings with double sets of doors and stairways, they still devote their lives to doing good and being good. And they continue to be as antiwar and socially aware as Shakers always have been. Not for many years have they taken in members or orphans, since the world now provides the welfare once offered by the Shakers. But they still love children, and a few little girls spend work vacations with them. Teen-age guides help out in the museum season, telling the Shaker adventure to tourists wandering through pristine restored rooms.

If the world is not yet ready for the good news that Mother Ann brought to America nearly 200 years ago, many thousands of people once were eager to receive it. Over the years, more than 70,000 men, women, and children dwelled among the Shakers and shared communal life on the model farms, although not all of them became members. And there is time, say these gentle Shaker sisters, for Shakerism or something akin to it to move and shake the world again.

To *Life* magazine, which pictured them as a dying sect and painted as grim a portrait of them as Charles Dickens once did, sprightly Sister Mildred wrote an indignant letter. "You missed the Brightness and Light which is Shakerism, the light, joy and vitality that is the product of Shakerism. Regardless of our numbers or our age, we have what the world is seeking and it will yet come into its own. What God has made alive will not stay buried."

The world surviving Mother Ann's children has inherited their many gifts. Out of the work of their hands has come a treasury of folk art, architecture, and music—an original American culture truly inspired by God and a way of life that was itself a religious service. Among other godsends were the gift to be simple and the gift of inspiration. The most important gift of all was the gift of community. Without it, the Shakers would have been just another American sect; with it, they became great. Like the Yankee communes whose stories follow this one, the Shakers with their successful "united interest" made communal life another and accepted American way.

CHAPTER III

The Rappites

A HUNDRED YEARS OF HARMONY

Every night a watchman walked the streets of a vine-covered village called Harmony. While the village slept, he cried this song:

Harken unto me, all ye people,
Midnight sounds from the steeple!
Twelve gates hath the city of gold,
Blest is he who enters the fold.

Again a day is passed
And a step nearer our end.
Our time runs out
And the joys of heaven are our reward.

At five A.M. a cowherd's horn blew to wake the towns-folk. Soon the men came out of their houses in bright blue jackets and wide trousers, and the women filed out of their houses in blue gowns, aprons, and straw bonnets. Off they marched to their jobs in fields and factories, singing to the tune of a band. They worked twelve hours, ate five meals, marched home, and went to bed by nine.

The end of which the watchman sang—the end of the world—had not come. Yet this is what the villagers lived for, without fear, for they believed they were a chosen people and would survive it. In the meantime, they purified themselves in preparation for the kingdom of God. They gave up tobacco, husbands and wives, and having families. Hard work for the common good brought wealth to all but luxury to none. The most comfortable life was enjoyed by their white-bearded preacher, a former vinegrower and weaver named George Rapp, who existed, he always told his congregation, only to present them personally to the Lord.

That is why they sold their farms and shops in Germany and pooled their money to follow their prophet to America. In 1803 Father Rapp and his son had crossed the sea to find a choice place to wait for Christ's Second Coming and a new beginning. They were overwhelmed at the size of America and decided to locate no farther west than Pennsylvania, where Germans had already found freedom of religion in some of America's earliest communes.

After buying 5,000 acres of "wild land" for $15,000 in the western part of the state, the Rapps wrote home that only the most courageous should join them. Despite this warning, 600 eager disciples, including the old and the poor, arrived in 1804 at the ports of Baltimore and Philadelphia. They gladly chose frontier dangers over the persecution they suffered in Württemberg for separating from the state Lutheran Church and heeding only the voice of God.

The followers of George Rapp were mostly farmers, vinetenders, and mechanics—sturdy pioneer types who were able to earn a living for themselves when they had to scatter that first hard fall and winter. Father Rapp himself, a tall strapping man of action as well as mystical visions and prophecies, set out with the hardiest workers to clear the new land twenty-five miles north of Pittsburgh, a dozen miles from the Ohio River on a main route to the West.

Portrait of George Rapp, founder of the Harmony Society, painted about 1836, when the patriarch was 79 or 80 years old.

An old street scene in Economy.

By spring there were log cabins ready to welcome the 125 families that came to serve God in a religious life together. They formed a "community of equality" and called it the Harmony Society to describe the harmonious way they proposed to live. Everyone contributed personal belongings and savings to a common fund, which amounted to $23,000, in the manner of the early Christians. In the strange new land with a different language and customs, where they had no friends among the "uncultured" people, there was protection and security, "care and consolation" for all who pledged to be readily and cheerfully obedient to "George Rapp and his associates." The ablest of these was Rapp's young disciple Frederick Reichert, whom he adopted and who led the flock to America.

After early hardships and poverty and the loss of many backsliding members, the community began to prosper. Each man and woman worked at a trade or in the households, cleared woodland, and planted grapevines. All sowed and reaped and hoed together. They were such a unified and unusual work force that they made the wilderness "blossom as the rose" and soon produced more than they needed. To travelers passing through the communal village, they sold surplus hides and shoes, cloth and flour, lumber and wooden ware. They sold them wagons to drive away in and harness for the horses. They also put on sale the whiskey they distilled, and the pioneers carried it to the West, where it became famous. The Rappites preferred wine and tended the new vineyards with care.

By 1810 the hard-working holy combination was in big business, the farmers and vinegrowers having learned how to mass-produce in a growing industrial market. They cultivated 2,000 acres, and a herdsman watched over a flock of fine merino sheep. Passing the time until the world would end, they accomplished more in five years than isolated families might have done in fifty.

A fresh revival of religion among them helped the Rappites' progress by strengthening their common goal and their immediate expectation of Jesus. To the chosen people in the American forest God's voice rang loud and clear. They felt his nearness and prepared for sainthood. It was necessary to be virgin pure to qualify for the kingdom of heaven on earth, when man's true nature, destroyed by the desire of Adam, would be restored. He would again become bisexual, man and woman in one in the image of God, as they saw him. Toward this destiny the society voted in 1807 to give up marriage and all sexual relations. They also gave up smoking, a great sacrifice.

During the first two years of communal living, many marriages had taken place, including that of Father Rapp's son John. But under the new law even recently married couples parted. So strong was the faith that husbands and wives continued to live in the same house as brothers and sisters. The men slept upstairs and the women downstairs, as they obeyed the biblical injunction that "they that had wives be as though they had none." Some members left the society when celibacy began, and got a refund on their contribution or a donation to help re-establish themselves in the new land.

Among those who stayed but were said to resist the ban on married life was John Rapp. His wife gave birth to a daughter, Gertrude, in 1808. When he died after an accident in 1812, a malicious, unfounded rumor arose in Pennsylvania and spread to Germany that he had been castrated by his father. Frederick became his heir. Father Rapp took his granddaughter into his household and gave her every advantage. John's grave was marked by the only monument in the burial ground, with its unmarked, identical resting places, and the stone received the favorite but rare decoration of the community, the Harmonist rose.

Although the system of celibacy promised future trouble, the village returned to normal and continued prosperity. A few years later the long haul of products to the river for market was considered a good reason for the brotherhood to move. Another was that its favorite crop, grapes, did poorly in Butler County, Pennsylvania. A third possible reason was a mystical one: George Rapp saw his pure society as symbolic of the "woman clothed with the sun" in the Book of Revelation, who fled to the wilderness, to "a place prepared by God," and would have to flee again and again. In 1814, therefore, the hamlet of Harmony was put up for sale. It sold at a good profit for $100,000, and a parcel of 30,000 fertile rolling acres on the Wabash River in Posey County, Indiana, was purchased for the society's second communal home.

Down the Ohio River in a flatboat went Father Rapp and an advance party of 100 farmers and mechanics to begin clearing dense forest land and building log cabins for another town named Harmony. A year later Frederick shepherded the rest of the members safely to Indiana, which was soon to become a state. Black locust trees were beginning to shade the streets of the well-planned village, enclosed by broad fields of grain, young green orchards, and sloping vineyards. The log cabins were replaced by six-room frame houses, each with its own dining room and a fireplace for cooking. Four three-story dormitories were also built. The dwellings had only a single door, on the side, leading to each household's flower and vegetable garden. A system of prefabricating the houses and maintaining "a hill of material" made it easier to build a town—and easier for the Rappites to move.

In the new village Father Rapp's brick house was prominent, with great verandas and a front entrance. Inside, it was uncarpeted and plain. His garden, which was for the enjoyment of all, was enhanced by exotic fruit trees—fig, orange, and lemon—and a heated greenhouse on wheels.

During the next five years steam power was introduced into the mills. The Rappites were soon able to manufacture everything needed on the frontier that formerly had to be imported from the East. And since they undercut their competition, the Mississippi Valley welcomed the flow from their brewery, brickyard, hattery, tannery, distillery, furnaces, and

The "Great House" of Father Rapp on the main street of Economy, Pennsylvania, was a showplace.

woolen mills, as well as the produce from the piggery and farms. Harmony, Indiana, became a shopping center for the entire region, with outlets and branch stores in Vincennes and Shawneetown and agents in big cities like St. Louis and New Orleans.

More labor was needed to nourish their enterprise. But because few Americans were attracted to the old-fashioned German colony with its monastic way of life, relatives and friends from the homeland migrated to Harmony in 1817 to fill the need. It was the same year that other Separatists fled Württemberg, following the Rappites' example, and founded a religious commune at Zoar, Ohio. The new Rappites slipped easily into the midwestern community, which remained more European than Yankee. Like Father Rapp, who never learned to speak English, the members still spoke German. They dressed in simple peasant costumes, and clung to Old World customs. The village was clean and picturesque and full of flowers.

It was a garden in the wilderness compared with other frontier towns at this time—poor, untidy trading posts like Evansville twenty miles away and half-Indian villages like Chicago. By 1820 Harmony was worth a million dollars. The willing, obedient followers of George Rapp through hard work had become astonishingly wealthy. They rarely left the borders of their backwoods utopia and had little in common with their neighbors.

Their poor Hoosier neighbors could not figure out the rich, thrifty foreigners in their midst. Mostly squatters living on other people's land, they considered the nonmarrying Rappites unnatural. "I studies and I studies on it," said a frontiersman who took his grain to their gristmill in Harmony.

But from afar Harmony caught the fancy of a poet. The famous Lord Byron wrote in the fifteenth canto of *Don Juan*:

> When Rapp the Harmonist embargo'd marriage
> In his harmonious settlement—(which flourishes
> Strangely enough as yet without miscarriage,
> Because it breeds no more mouths than it nourishes,
> Without those sad expenses which disparage
> What Nature naturally most encourages)—
> Why call'd he "Harmony" a state sans wedlock?
> Now here I have got the preacher at a dead lock.
>
> Because he either meant to sneer at harmony
> Or marriage, by divorcing them thus oddly.
> But whether reverend Rapp learn'd this in Germany
> Or no, 't is said his sect is rich and godly,
> Pious and pure, beyond what I can term any
> Of ours, although they propagate more broadly.
> My objection's to his title, not his ritual,
> Although I wonder how it grew habitual.

Some other Englishmen had a closer view. Twenty miles up the Wabash River on the Illinois side there was a co-operative settlement of English farmers. Although they often visited Harmony, bringing travelers from abroad, they disapproved of the slavish quality of life there and claimed the people were governed by a "disgusting superstition." The great financial success of the Rappites did not impress them, since it was the obvious result of plenty of money to invest and a large supply of unquestioning captive workers.

Visitors could see, however, that the 700 Rappites, busy and bossed from dawn to dark, were contented. Carrying out God's will, they had improved their condition, rising from poor farmers to rich American businessmen and land-owners. If they sacrificed private property and personal freedom, they were satisfied with what they had—security, company, and spiritual guidance. Evidently they did not mind being treated like children, regulated like clocks, and called "Rapp's serfs" by many Americans, since they worked harmoniously together for twenty-five years before there was any division among them. They fully believed God had called them and given them the truth and that their society had been formed under his special direction. They had no doubt that their life was the best preparation for his kingdom, which was near at hand. The brotherly love among them would ease the transition to heaven. Therefore, they would work and wait and please God with their lives until the end.

For this reason Harmony lived up to its name. Few invaded its sanctity. There were no attacks by Indians, no threats from river pirates. No need arose for shooting through the long loopholes built into the church and granary. Not once did anyone flee for protection into the long underground passages beneath the fields. Among the Rappites themselves, there were no troublemakers, no nonconformists. Unlike most men, they knew exactly where they were going and never expected to alter their course, although it turned out that some of them did.

Cautioned by their pastor against greed, "none cared overmuch for riches." The shoemaker made new shoes when the old ones wore out. The tailor provided patches. There was little outward change, and little inward change could be observed among these pious people through all the years they waited. Led by two extraordinary men, they pursued their harmonious, unpretentious way, living by the Bible, especially the Book of Acts and the Book of Revelation. They seldom wrote about themselves, and, because of the language barrier, far less was written and known about them than about the more democratic and articulate Shakers.

The great pleasure of the Rappites, as with most German people, was music. They preferred band music and singing, mostly hymns and psalms. Father Rapp and Frederick wrote many hymns for special occasions, passionate odes praising nature and the virgin St. Sophia, symbol of the spiritual wisdom sought by Rappites. These were the special features of the *Harmoniefests*, or feasts, which celebrated the holy days and the Lord's Supper, the gathering of the harvest, and the anniversary of the founding of the society in 1805. The only national holiday observed was the Fourth of July, which happily coincided with another Rappite anniversary, the arrival of some of the original members in America on July 4, 1804. On this occasion, therefore, they sometimes invited their American friends on the Wabash over for a big patriotic party, with speeches, dinner, and beer. The other Harmony feasts were private and sometimes were postponed until Father Rapp or Frederick returned from a business trip. For days ahead the food was prepared in great kettles in the big common kitchen of the Feast Hall, which was like the town hall in the homeland. The typical menu offered a specialty of veal, rice, pears, and ginger cookies, served with great mugs of the best wines, and cider.

Aside from these feasts, there was little excitement in the lives of the diligent Rappites. Father Rapp heard them confess their few sins, which, if unrepented, disturbed the harmony of the community and the universe. He visited them when they were sick, healed them if he could with folk medicines, or buried them with plainness and lack of ceremony in the orchard burial ground called God's Acre. There, it was believed, they would sleep in the white shrouds made for the Second Coming, when they would be raised up to meet Jesus. Father Rapp settled all arguments that arose in the house of peace, even though ill temper was discouraged. On week-day evenings he offered group counseling in religious matters to separate gatherings of different ages and sexes. On Sundays he preached twice to a divided congregation of men and women, who entered the church through separate doors as soon as the bell rang and later left it—ladies first—without dawdling.

On the farms and in the shops women were the equals of men and worked side by side with them. Sometimes, swing-ing sickles, they helped to harvest as much as 100 acres in a single day, an achievement that earned special wine at *ves-perbrot*, their midafternoon lunch and singing break.

In the distant outlying fields where they labored together the Rappites were overseen by their leader. Sometimes he used a megaphone to prod and direct crews. The English farmers accused him of playing on the field workers' Old World superstitions by means of the underground tunnels and passageways. He was said to use the entrances and exits to emerge suddenly, and then disappear, in the middle of a cornfield or potato patch. There, six feet tall and wearing his customary peaked cap, he seemed like a boulder or bush that would mysteriously fade away.

It was also claimed that he appeared by the same under-ground route at the platform of the church, where he preached loudly in German about the approaching doomsday. Once, with fanfare, he produced a great limestone slab with giant footprints embedded in it. He said that it was found along the Mississippi River bank at St. Louis. Although he may only have speculated about the supernatural size of the footprints, hearsay attributed them directly to the angel Gabriel, whom the spiritual leader was supposed to have met while he was meditating.

The stately, blue-eyed patriarch with the long snowy beard (the first full beard in the society) inspired his followers by his own example of constant hard work. He believed, as did Mother Ann of the Shakers and John Humphrey Noyes of the Oneida Community, that physical toil—especially hard field work—was the cure for most spiritual and bodily ills. When not busy on the farms, helping the plowmen or harvesters, or in the mills, advising and teaching his people, he studied botany, geology, astronomy, and mechanics, and kept up with the latest religious writings from Germany. He even dabbled in alchemy, the medieval science that tried to extract gold from base metals. If one could turn ordinary mortals into perfect saints, why not common metals into gold? Even the more reasonable Frederick was said to share this unlikely and worldly interest.

Among the men and women he would have perfect, the word of the elder Rapp was law. "Father Rapp says it" was enough to satisfy any member on any issue. His followers automatically waited for him to tell them what to do and how to do it because, they said, he knew everything. Young people especially loved him and listened when he told them how to be good. "When I met him in the street, if I had a bad thought in my head, it flew away," one youth said. "He was a man before whom no evil could stand." And when he warned them to beware of luxury and self-love, saying, "To inherit heaven, you must give up the earth," most Rappites were ready to do so.

Many outsiders, on the other hand, called the magnetic preacher a tyrant, a dictator, and a slave driver. Some critics could not reconcile Father Rapp's strenuous insistence on following Christ in the ways of love with his deep involvement in the whiskey business. The Quakers, moreover, accused him of driving hard bargains when he hired white "redemptioners" on ships in the port of Philadelphia. He was said to take advantage of the immigrants' need for work in order to pay their passage at the end of the voyage to America. Some, however, called him a good man and told this story to prove it.

Once in the early days of the Harmony Society, Father Rapp went to Pittsburgh for supplies and was refused credit. At the river bank where he wept and prayed, "for the need was great and their means at the time were small," a merchant found him and asked what was the matter.

"Being informed, he offered Father Rapp two four-horse wagonloads of provisions, telling him also to borrow no trouble about the payment. The thrifty Communists were blessed immediately with bountiful crops, and soon paid the debt. Years rolled by," writes William Alfred Hinds in *American Communities*. "The Harmonists prospered in all their enterprises; and when a great financial hurricane swept over the land, they stood erect while many houses toppled over. In the midst of the storm they learned that the merchant who had so generously befriended them in their day of trouble was now himself unable to meet his obligations and threatened with financial ruin.

"Father Rapp welcomed the opportunity it offered. Filling his saddle-bags with solid coin, he rode to Pittsburgh, found his old benefactor, poured out his money before him, and told him he could have as much more if it were needed; and so the merchant was saved!"

The Rappites' other great leader, Frederick Rapp, was a less controversial and different sort of man. He was their business manager and politician, but also their poet. He seemed less concerned with the heavenly glories to come than the opportunity and beauty at hand. Frederick tried to brighten the routine life in Harmony by encouraging public pleasures like band concerts and placing fresh flowers on the machines in the factories. A musician, who composed some of the society's favorite hymns, he was a skilled architect and stonecutter by trade. His good taste and imagination gave much of the character and charm to the Rappite villages. He designed the famous labyrinth or maze—an ancient mystical symbol of life itself—that surrounded a hidden resting place with miles of winding paths. He carved the Harmonist rose, seen by Father Rapp in a vision, over the main entrance to the stone church. Beside it, cut into the stone, was the biblical inscription, in Luther's version, "Unto you will come the golden rose." The rose was a symbol of the Millennium.

It was a remarkable church, shaped like a cross. Plans for it were supposed to have been delivered from the heavens. Whatever the inspiration, it was an ambitious project for a simple people who sometimes liked to worship outdoors and who never rushed into church building after founding their villages. Visitors were surprised to see in the wilds of Indiana a church that stretched 120 feet in each direction and contained many aisles, plus a circle of twenty-eight huge polished columns of native black walnut, cherry, and sassafras woods. Years later, after the Rappites sold their property and moved a third time, they bought back the cruciform church on the Wabash and tore it down except for one wing of the cross, which contained Frederick's doorway. With the salvaged brick a thick protective wall was built around the old

The Rappites' favorite decoration, the rose, used here on a newel post in the Great House, Economy, Pennsylvania.

burying ground with its rows of nameless graves among the apple trees.

As gifted in finance as in the fine arts, Frederick traveled about as the business representative of the Rappites and dealt with many prominent people. He received several political assignments, helped frame the constitution of Indiana and locate its capitol.

The state of Indiana was sorry to lose such a productive people when the Rapps decided to move again. But this time they intended to go back to the more civilized East instead of further west toward America's new frontiers. In Indiana the Rappites suffered greatly from "the fever and ague," or malaria, and were surrounded by envious neighbors. One of the Englishmen in the nearby colony, Richard Flower, was offered a commission of five thousand dollars to sell Harmony abroad. He was returning to England with his son George because the younger man's life had been threatened by Illinois slaveowners. They feared he was planning a community for emancipated slaves because he rented land to free Negroes. He had also freed twenty-five slaves by buying them and sending them to Haiti.

Only a utopian would buy a used utopia. Robert Owen, who owned a famous model factory town called New Lanark in Scotland, happened to be in the market for just such a property as Harmony. Since correcting some of the horrors of early capitalism—child labor and the sixteen-hour day—in his New Lanark mills, the great reformer had been making plans for a "new moral order" among men. He had already exchanged views with George Rapp, although they hardly agreed, for Owen was not a religious man. Harmony, how-

Robert Owen bought the entire Rappite communal village of Harmony, Indiana, to establish his own community of workers.

ever, excited the hopes of all reformers and social improvers. It was showing the world that the co-operation of a united communal group could lead to influence and success.

In 1825 Mr. Owen got a bargain when Harmony was sold to him for $150,000. His "New Harmony" got a head start by inheriting all the Rappite improvements—houses, dormitories, factories, farms, orchards, vineyards, stores, furnaces, livestock, the wharf, and even the town clock and bells. Nonetheless, his workingman's paradise—America's first nonreligious social utopia—lasted only a few turbulent years.

Meanwhile, the Rappites moved in their usual methodical fashion to 3,000 acres on the Ohio River, eighteen miles from Pittsburgh and only fifteen miles from their original American home. The new town was called Economy instead of Harmony III, as if to confirm their own hard-earned place in the divine economy or plan for heaven and earth. Here, further expansion continued the uncommon success of those who had united for nobler goals.

Unlike the other Rappite towns, Economy became an important and a popular stopping place on the stagecoach route. It was a quaint and appealing village with an attractive and lucrative inn. Its wide, even streets were planted with shade trees, and on a bluff overlooking the town, benches were arranged for enjoying the river view. The plain red brick dwellings appeared to be banded with green, as grapevines for special-occasion wines grew on trellises on their warm sunny sides.

In Economy, Frederick created another green maze and grotto in which the Rappites could lose themselves. They also enjoyed a deer park and goldfish pond. On a more cultural level, a museum for art and natural objects was founded by Frederick in the Feast Hall. From New York and Philadelphia he brought paintings and collections of rare minerals, shells, birds, insects, and Indian relics.

Of course, the Great House of Father Rapp on the main street was the finest. It faced the church, and its lavish garden was open to the public. Band concerts were held there on Sunday afternoons and summer evenings as the sun went down. The house was well-furnished, and its table was set with fine china and burnished silver. In those days a servant set out fancy food, for the community attracted much attention, its prosperity commending it to a stream of distinguished visitors.

Such a visitor announced himself by a letter from abroad in 1829. Count Maximilian de Leon, calling himself Ambassador of God, descendant from the stem of Judah and the root of David, requested an audience with the "Aged Patriarch George Rapp and his Associated Superintendents and Society." He was seeking advice on establishing in America a scriptural or Bible-based communism like theirs. Father Rapp was impressed by the count's ancestry and by his own apparent worldwide fame. He replied that he would be happy to receive the count.

One bright day in the fall of 1831 the excited citizens of Economy lined the streets. They wore their Sunday garments of silk, home-grown, home-reeled and spun and woven in their own silk mills. Music flowed from the band stationed on the church tower as a coach approached the village inn and Father Rapp hurried out to greet it.

Out stepped an elegant gentleman, splendidly dressed for the role he was playing and carrying a "golden book." He was not a count but a European adventurer, religious fanatic, and fraud.

"This meeting," he proclaimed to the awed congregation waiting for him at the church, "is the most important event since the Creation. Henceforth, all the troubles and sorrows of the Lord's people will cease." He was wrong. The troubles of this sheltered people had just begun.

The count and the forty foreign disciples who attended him put on a grand show. It was a long time before Father Rapp, shrewd and dramatic as he was, realized that he was entertaining a rival prophet. By then the visitors had settled into five houses and the inn for the winter. For some reason they were never turned out. The count boldly spent his time investigating everything in the community from its unused cradles to its unidentified graves. He asked searching questions that worried the older members and shocked the young. No one had questioned authority before.

The count was no democrat, but he loudly championed the Americans' right to the pursuit of happiness, including marriage, more comfort, and less work. He said he was divinely sent to right their wrongs under George Rapp and to replace him as their leader. What was probably most effective in his campaign against Father Rapp was his claim to possession of the philosopher's stone and the ability to turn worthless metal into gold. Leon boasted of having a fortune and great treasures for a new City of God that he would build. Finally, he challenged Rapp to a showdown.

A vote was called to decide which leader the Rappites should follow. "A greater number of good people," represented by 500 ballots, favored Father Rapp and the old order of things, and 250 votes went to Count Leon. When he learned the results, Father Rapp wryly quoted from the Bible's Book of Revelation: "And the tail of the serpent drew the third part of the stars of heaven, and did cast them to the earth."

He was eager to be rid of the count and his converts, and agreed to pay $105,000 in installments—an immense sum for those days—if they would leave Economy within three months. They were allowed to take their clothing and household goods but would have no further claim to communal property. The count himself was to be gone within three weeks.

When he finally left, Leon hovered nearby planning a competing community that would permit marriage. He located it only ten miles down the river on 800 acres of land. In the end, only 176 converts joined him and his New Philadelphia Society at Phillipsburg. They quickly squandered the money given them and learned that Leon had no more. In desperation they tried to plunder the storehouses of Economy and take over the Great House. But their former brothers and sisters, as well as neighbors, were ready for them with barricades and drove them out of town, typically, to fife and drum. After the unsuccessful raid, the Leonites fled down the Ohio River and never returned.

Some of the deserters later joined another German commune in Bethel, Missouri, under the leadership of Dr. William Keil. One ex-Rappite became a member of the Mormon community, going the gamut from no wife to several, as allowed by the Latter-day Saints. But most of Leon's disciples followed him down the Mississippi to Louisiana, where he searched for gold and waited in a high place for the Second

Main Street, Economy, Pennsylvania, in 1883, the only place in the village where the "world's people" were allowed to circulate freely. The young man is John Duss, who lived as a child among the Rappites and later returned to help them when they declined. On the hill behind the town is an oil well, one of the Rappites' many profitable industrial undertakings. Houses lining the street are banded with green, where grapevines grow on the brick.

Coming of the Lord in America. The next year the count died of cholera. And the remnant that remained loyal to him moved on to establish Germantown, Louisiana, which lasted about thirty-six years.

The Harmony Society was never the same again. Father Rapp said that the trials and tribulations they had suffered were tests to see if they were worthy of God. But Frederick regretted the loss of so many younger members and remained deeply troubled. "Nothing," he had once said, "could disturb their harmony," but something had. From then on he and Father Rapp shared an uneasy partnership at the head of the shrunken group. There had been friction between them before, when the elder leader had welcomed back a pair of lovers who had eloped. He had even asked the society to pray for them. No such charity was ever shown the others. Frederick knew—and feared that the society also knew—of Father Rapp's partiality for the young runaway woman who had worked with him in his laboratory. There were other tensions over Father Rapp's tightening of his authority and insistence that the members sign once again the founding principles of the society. Eventually their differences were reconciled. But the strain of the Leon affair wearied and weakened Frederick, and led to the untimely death in 1834 of the prophet's second son.

Frederick's loss was a great blow to the society; from the beginning it had leaned heavily on him. In a funeral speech a trustee called his death "a violent break in the chain of brotherhood." But, he added, "we will not become either weary or lax in the battle, but the more firmly united, that the bond of brotherly love and friendship be still more closely drawn."

In spite of everything, Economy went on prospering far beyond George Rapp's dreams of what would come to pass for his uncorrupted people. Early in the 1840's a religious revival convinced him that the Second Coming and the new beginning were at last at hand. From that time on he kept everything in readiness for the great event that he expected to witness. Many of his followers believed he would never die. But in 1847, at the age of ninety, the old patriarch weakened and took to his bed.

One Sunday, after addressing his sorrowful congregation from the window of his room, he was heard to murmur, "If I did not so fully believe that the Lord has designed me to place our Society before his presence, I should think my last moments had come." One by one those who had remained faithful to him filed past his bed, and he bid each a separate farewell before he died.

They were stunned by his death. Many expected him to come back to keep his promise, and to this end they continued in brotherhood and faith. They went on living simply and chastely in their quiet communal households, obeying less charismatic masters. Nine elders, of whom two became trustees, managed their souls and their incredible wealth. Even as their numbers dwindled, they became multimillionaires. Oil and coal had been discovered on some of their distant landholdings, and they owned vast tracts of real estate that they never saw, and large profitable investments in railroads they never rode. Although a number of legal battles were waged against them by ex-members claiming money, the courts upheld the society.

In the 1850's there was talk of merging with two other

The last two members of the Harmony Society in the Great House garden.

religious communes that lived a life apart—the German Separatists at Zoar and the Shakers. With the Shakers the Rappites shared the principles of celibacy and community of goods. But after reading some Shaker tracts they were reluctant to combine with such religious radicals. Shaker Elder Henry C. Blinn, however, had a more moving explanation when he wrote, "Their reason for not uniting with the Shakers was that all the little places on the earth where purity is the object are like so many flowers, though of different hues, yet all are beautiful in the sight of the heavenly Father. And that they were one of these flowers in the great boquet. If they moved from the place where they reside, they would lose their identity and be lost from the boquet, and if this was made of all white, all yellow, all blue or any other color, it would not be so pretty as though it was variegated."

Gradually, well before the close of the nineteenth century, the vigor of the Rappites waned. They grew too few and too old to drive the wheels and run the looms and wine presses and the Golden Rule Distillery. There was no one to replace them, and the local industries shut down. The aging members lived on the income from their investments, and Economy grew quiet as Sunday. Down its shaded cobblestoned streets ambled an occasional stout old man in a bright blue jacket, who tipped his broad-brimmed hat to a stranger, or an ample old woman in a blue gown and high cap, who murmured "*Guten Tag.*" As the number of strollers dwindled, the need arose for someone to straighten out their complicated financial problems. John Duss, a man whom the society had raised as a child, was invited back to help them. He could not restore the old Harmony spirit or fortune, but he was able to salvage enough to keep the Rappites secure and without fear until their deaths.

The Harmony Society was dissolved in 1905, after 100 years of existence. One member survived until 1921. None of the Old World German sects that came to the New World lasted longer. None did more to help America expand. Working for a heavenly society, this businesslike company of believers built three frontier towns, helped develop two states, and produced an industrial empire.

CHAPTER IV

The Oneida Community

✝ ✝✝ ✝✝✝ ✝✝✝✝✝ ✝✝✝✝✝✝✝✝✝ ✝✝✝✝✝✝✝✝✝✝✝✝✝✝✝✝✝✝✝✝

FAR OUT IN THE 1840's

We will build us a dome
On our beautiful plantation,
And we'll all have one home,
And one family relation

sang the Oneida Community. And what a strange relation it was for a holy family: every man was the husband of every woman, and every woman was the wife of every man. The community called the system "complex marriage"; the world called it free love and never saw Oneida as the deeply religious, carefully regulated way of life that it was.

Yet these men and women considered themselves "saints." Their passionate faith led them to think they were sinless when they pooled their affections along with their property in total communism under God. To them what was *really* wicked was the world's way of romantic attachment to one person. That was *selfish* love. The community cured it and other misdemeanors by mutual criticism, a kind of plain speaking. The brothers and sisters gathered around and talked the guilty ones into self-improvement. And they were not allowed to talk back.

This was such an effective system that it kept peace in the communal family, which dwelled together for thirty years in a big mansion in upstate New York. Under Oneida's "law of love," criticism was the sole method of discipline, and it was a health cure as well.

When anyone was sick, he called for a committee instead of a doctor. A group of six or eight members came to criticize him. They told him his faults and pointed out the weakest points in his conduct and character. What they told him was often so perceptive that it threw the patient into a sweat. This supposedly drove the "disease-spirit" out of his body, and he usually got well. In the mid-nineteenth century, this group-marrying, self-doctoring community knew that illness can be caused by personality problems, and sometimes the desire for attention.

Special attention was something not even the children in this unusual family got, even though they were the "dearest" communal project of all. Instead of receiving the close concentration of two parents, the children shared in the interest of more than 200. Babies over fifteen months and boys and girls up to twelve lived in the separate Children's House, connected by an underground passage to the big house. They were raised by members who were experts in child care and had the "best talent and most taste" for it. This left their mothers free to work and study, and eager to be visited by their children a few times a week.

Although many of the children were named Noyes, some had different mothers. They were born after an extraordinary experiment in human breeding. Their father was someone special. He was John Humphrey Noyes, the founder of the Oneida Community, the man who had set these people apart.

Noyes was a red-headed, square-jawed, strong-minded

The Mansion House.

Yankee from a prominent Vermont family. His father was a rich country banker who once tutored Daniel Webster and later represented the State of Vermont in Congress. On his mother's side he was related to Rutherford B. Hayes, nineteenth President of the United States.

In 1831, when Noyes was a twenty-year-old Dartmouth College graduate studying law in Putney, Vermont, one of the greatest revivals of the century was at its height. The religious excitement was so contagious that even though young Noyes was skeptical he went along with the crowd when a revival preacher swept into town and everyone flocked to hear him.

John Humphrey Noyes, who believed that "when the will of God is done on earth as it is in Heaven, there will be no marriage."

In those times a revival meeting could last for days and sometimes weeks, overwhelming sinners with terror and joy and casting a spell that disrupted entire towns. This meeting lasted four days and nights, shrill with the wails and "audible groaning" of women, who were allowed a voice at these "radical" meetings while they were required to be silent in orthodox churches. At the climax young John Noyes found himself down front on the "anxious seat," where he was dramatically reborn and "saved." The mystical experience of his conversion changed his life and career. In his diary he wrote: "Hitherto the world, henceforth God!" He dropped the law and hurried into the ministry, to the delight of his devout mother.

Religious training, however, turned out to be much less exciting than a revival. At Andover Seminary, Noyes found only a few ardent friends among his fellow students who shared his fervor and who swore with him to remain "young converts forever." In their eagerness to improve themselves, they told each other their faults and forced themselves to accept painful criticism without flinching and in silence. It was here that Noyes learned the potential of mutual criticism. But Andover was too conservative for the young zealot, and he could not decide whether to stay. Opening his Bible at random one day, he read this passage: "Fear not ye: for I know that ye seek Jesus, which was crucified. He is not here."

Accepting this as a divine direction, he left his friends the next year, promising to join them in missionary work after graduation, and transferred to the theological school at Yale. The atmosphere was more liberal, but he was not at home with the religion taught there, not even by Professor Nathaniel W. Taylor, who questioned the established Calvinist doctrine of original sin. Dr. Taylor claimed that infants were born sinless and could not sin until they did so voluntarily and were responsible for their actions. Taylor's compromise and his faith in man's ability to fulfill God's expectations of good encouraged John Noyes to go much further in the matter of sin—in fact, to excuse man from it altogether.

Noyes had arrived, as he put it, at "a new experience and new views of the way of salvation, which took the name of *Perfectionism.*" This was the bold religious doctrine, advanced by the popular revivals, which said that man could reach a state of perfection in this life without waiting for the next.

So excited was the young student minister about "perfect holiness" that he changed his mind about becoming a missionary abroad and decided to save New England first. In New Haven, Noyes had joined one of the new "free churches," which were more experimental and open-minded than the Congregational Church of his parents and other conventional denominations. In that liberated atmosphere he felt free to climb to the pulpit after he received his license to preach and announce his own emancipation from sin.

"I am perfect!" he cried on February 20, 1834, a date celebrated as a major holiday by the Oneida Community. This outburst dismayed the clergymen who had just ordained him. In vain he tried to explain that perfection only meant having "a pure heart and a good conscience toward God." One still had to work for perfect behavior but was freed from the dreary process of having to repent and sin and repent again all one's life.

Noyes based his views on his own interpretation of the New Testament, pointing out a passage that proved to him that the Second Coming of Christ had taken place at the time of the destruction of Jerusalem in A.D. 70: "Verily I say unto you, there be some standing here which shall not taste death till they see the Son of Man coming in his Kingdom." Since that time, he declared, the world had been in readiness for the kingdom of God and the perfection of earthly life. Men could be as sinless as the Apostle Paul and members of the primitive church.

To his teachers Noyes's talk of immediate salvation from sin flaunted the moral law. Such heresy, called "antinomianism," could not be permitted, and they revoked his license to preach. Most of Noyes's associates agreed that he had gone too far, and some even considered him insane.

This left John Humphrey Noyes an outcast at the age of only twenty-three. If the church had not expelled him, he might have continued his interest in the antislavery or temperance movements, two causes in the mainstream of popular reform. Instead, he now put freedom from sin and unbelief ahead of every other issue. Slavery would automatically cease, he wrote to his friend, the abolitionist William Lloyd Garrison, when "perfect holiness" put an end to vice and evil.

Over the next dozen years Noyes continued to preach Perfectionism in its most extreme form and in defiance of the ministry that had rejected his services. "I have taken away their license to sin," he said, "yet they keep on sinning. So, they have taken away my license to preach, yet I shall go on preaching!" He grew more and more revolutionary, becoming one of the most radical crusaders against the Establishment of his times. He attacked not only the "sin system" but the "marriage system," the "work system," and the "death system." No government bound him except God's.

His doctrine of holiness attracted a small admiring following among the scattered and unorganized groups of men and women who had embraced Perfectionism after the great revival.* He traveled throughout New York and New England, visiting and reassuring his disciples of emancipation through perfect faith. Believers in Vermont, New York, Massachusetts, and New Jersey began to look to him for leadership. They read everything he wrote in a journal called the *Perfectionist,* looked forward to his correspondence and to his appearance at regional conventions of Perfectionists, where his novel ideas were controversial. Competing for leadership in the movement, he challenged the more moderate Charles Grandison Finney, the great revivalist preacher who had come out of the West, conquered New York, invaded conservative New England, and "carried the fire to Boston."

During this period of his life, Noyes was as much at odds with himself as with the times. For one thing, he was rejected in love. One of his first converts to Perfectionism at the New Haven Free Church was Abigail Merwin, who was frightened away by his extremism. When she married someone else in 1837, Noyes followed her to Ithaca, New York, vowing to abolish the tyranny of the marriage system that separated them.

---

* One of Noyes's disciples in the Midwest was Luther Guiteau of Illinois, who encouraged his son to join the Oneida Community when it was formed. Charles Guiteau was a misfit and an unstable, unpopular member of the community. He left Oneida to complete an insane "mission"—the assassination of President James Garfield in 1881.

In a letter to a friend soon after, which later became notorious, he confided his views on marrying: "When the will of God is done on earth as it is in heaven, *there will be no marriage.* The marriage supper of the Lamb is a feast at which every dish is free to every guest. Exclusiveness, jealousy, quarreling, have no place there, for the same reason as that which forbids the guests at a thanksgiving dinner to claim each his separate dish and quarrel with the rest for his rights. In a holy community there is no more reason why sexual intercourse should be restrained by law, than why eating and drinking should be—and there is as little occasion for shame in the one case as in the other. God has placed a wall of partition between the male and female during the apostasy, for good reasons, which will be broken down in the resurrection for equally good reasons. But woe to him who abolishes the law of the apostasy before he stands in the holiness of the resurrection [i.e., conversion to Perfectionism].

"The guests of the marriage supper may have each his favorite dish, each a dish of his own procuring, and that without the jealousy of exclusiveness. I call a certain woman my wife—she is yours, she is Christ's, and in him she is the bride of all saints. She is dear in the hand of a stranger, and according to my promise to her I rejoice. My claim upon her cuts directly across the marriage covenant of this world, and God knows the end."

In the end he recovered from his passion, although his views on marriage did not alter. A few months after it was written, the letter on perfect love found its way out of private hands into a religious journal. From there it was picked up with relish by the general press—which disregarded his emphatic condition of holiness—and exploded into a national scandal. Many of Noyes's converts dropped away at the disclosure. And many virtuous Perfectionists who would never "meddle with anyone's wife" saw their religion "swallowed up by the Devil."

Perfectionism was a faith that invited scandal even before John Humphrey Noyes made his unique contribution to it. In the wake of the revivals, some felt so emancipated from sin that they took liberties in their behavior. Noyes disapproved of the tendency to disrupt marriage and take "spiritual wives," sometimes one after another. In some groups the practice of holy kissing and holding hands at religious meetings led to sexual promiscuity.

Once, in subzero New England weather, Noyes himself fled temptation. A pair of attractive female Perfectionists pursued him to his bedroom after an ardent meeting. They wanted only to "bundle" in bed, but their minister escaped them, plunging through deep snow sixty miles back to his home in Putney. After that, adventurous Perfectionist circles condemned John Noyes for his holier-than-thou attitude. But he was only trying to protect his own reputation and the reputation of the religion.

To stop tongues still wagging about his marriage letter, Noyes even decided to take a bride. But first he made one of the strangest proposals in history. When he asked for her hand, he assured Miss Harriet Holton that marriage would not limit the range of their affections! "I desire and expect my yoke-fellow will love all who love God with a warmth, a strength of affection which is unknown to earthly lovers, and as freely as if she stood in no particular connection with me," wrote John Noyes.

Harriet, a true disciple who also offered essential financial support, promptly accepted. After their wedding in June, 1838, the couple settled down on John's family farm in Vermont. He had already converted all his relatives except his father, who nonetheless left him a comfortable inheritance. At Putney they and a few others formed the nucleus for the holy community that Noyes's Perfectionist principles called forth.

With a secondhand printing press, the family group learned to set type and began to produce publications that spread Noyes's influence and kept his disciples informed of his latest views. A general store was opened, and the public was invited to worship in the chapel built by the family. The neighbors came to trade and to attend Noyes's Bible school. For years they accepted the small religious commune that shared farm chores and storekeeping, studied three hours a day, and took meals together. To the Vermonters the simplicity of the eating arrangements seemed the most remarkable thing about the community. Breakfast was the only hot meal served by the women; they left a variety of provisions in the pantry for self-service the rest of the day. This was intended to free women from "the worst kind of slavery," as well as contribute to general health.

During these experimental years Harriet Noyes bore five children and lost four of them. Her husband longed to spare her and all women from such pain and from a life restricted to constant childbirth and child-rearing. The system of birth control he invented accomplished that salvation. It also made his social theory of group marriage possible.

Complex marriage, as Noyes called it, was not practiced by the Putney community until Noyes taught the men how to safeguard the women. When the Perfectionists formally adopted Bible communism in 1845, they took the final step out of marriage. By then membership in the group had grown, despite the dropouts that occurred when Noyes introduced the uncomfortable discipline of mutual criticism. New members contributed what they had to the common resources, but the major communal support came from Noyes's patrimony and his wife's. Gradually the separate households merged, and complex marriage, at first in "quartette form," began. A new social order was under way, one that respected women's rights and rejected the "selfish ownership" of them in marriage.

When the respectable people of Putney learned about "larger relationships" than husband and wife at the Noyes farm, they were outraged. They sent their daughters away for safekeeping and tried to get rid of the shameful commune in their midst. Noyes was arrested and charged with adultery as well as illegal faith-healing, which had resulted, in one case, in a woman's death.

He protested, "The communism of love you persecute us for is the beauty and glory of heaven!" He argued that philosophers, and not small-town officials, should decide the guilt. Still, the Yankee prophet saw no point in being run out of town or becoming a martyr. Forfeiting $2,000 bail, he fled from Vermont in 1847 to the state of New York, where a larger group of believers later gathered around him. First he went to New York City and there received an invitation from a small communal settlement of Perfectionist families upstate to relocate the Putney group and join them. Noyes inspected the land, former Indian territory, and carefully explained complex marriage before he accepted.

In midwinter of 1848 the Putney family—thirty-one

adults and fourteen children—straggled over the border to join him at Oneida in Madison County, New York. The property there was run down, with only a shabby log cabin or two and an old saw mill on Oneida Creek. But Noyes saw "some romance in beginning our community in the log huts of the Indians." Besides, the silent wilderness and sheltering hills promised tolerance for a home "in which each is married to all, and where love is honored and cultivated."

The western New York region was known as the "burned-over district." It had been a revival center, famous for fiery religious and social "enthusiasms." Communities of Shakers and Owenites and phalanxes of Fourierites had been established there. In this area the Mormons had come into being and the Millerites had waited for the end of the world. Visions of perfection still smoldered after the spectacular revivals and experiments in the twenties, thirties, and forties, and almost as many New Yorkers as Yankees rallied round the Putney refugees to give life to still another dream. In 1849 there were eighty-seven members on the small patch of land; only two years later there were 205. Housing was a problem as new recruits came from both high and humble social positions to join the Oneida Community. They left farms, foundries, shops, businesses, classrooms, courtrooms, and pulpits to build a heaven on earth where all who accepted the gospel according to John Humphrey Noyes could be saints.

But utopia was not built in a day, and even a spiritual community had to eat. Despite the "special providence" and divine inspiration on which Noyes counted, many years of hard work and slow moral improvement lay ahead. He himself worked as a mason on the big single dwelling designed for the new style of living. The women also shared in manual labor, completing most of the interior lathing of the Mansion House, as it was called. They shared the care of children as well, and since birth control was one of their founding religious principles, they postponed having babies until the community could afford them.

When they were hampered by their long dresses while working, the community women invented a new costume. They shortened their skirts to the calf and used the extra material to make slim straight pantalets or trousers to wear underneath. They also bobbed their long heavy hair, not only to save time and trouble, but to discourage vanity. Both styles won the approval of John Noyes. He thought women in long skirts looked like butter churns on casters. The public was shocked by the new fashions, which were considered unfeminine. Another example of the extremes to which these "free lovers" went!

From the beginning free love was a constant charge against the community. It made John Noyes snort. "Free love! That terrible combination of two very good ideas, freedom and love!" He claimed to have originally invented the term in the Putney school to describe "the social state of heaven." As any father must do, he defended his family, insisting, "The tie that binds us together is as permanent and sacred as that of marriage, for it is our *religion*. We receive no members who don't give heart and hand to the family interest for life and forever."

The members resented the accusations, too. They shared with Noyes a sense of a pure and special state, a belief that they alone possessed, through him, certain sacred truths. Their

The Oneida family at dinner.

home, they believed, was a branch of the kingdom of heaven. They were sure that the world, which they saw as sinners critical of saints, would some day copy the Oneida system. In the meantime, safe from sin and greedy competition, the family was harmonious and happy even before it reached financial success and won the grudging respect of the nation.

For their livelihood the Perfectionists experimented in a whole series of occupations. Farming and logging were not enough to support them. As a student of the American community movement, Noyes noted that too many groups failed through their dependence on agriculture alone. He was all for Yankee tinkering at one manufactory or another until one or more succeeded.

At first Oneida products were boycotted, even though neighbors bringing wood to their sawmill reported that the Perfectionists were hardworking and not objectionable at all. Before long, New York State housewives relented and bought the quality fruits and vegetables that the women of the community put up in some of the first glass jars. The Oneida peddlers, also, brought back praise for the good craftsmanship of the traveling bags, satchels, straw hats, mop holders, brooms, and rustic furniture turned out by the members, who often worked together with the children in "bees," while one person read a book aloud.

They were full of enterprise and enthusiasm. When customers asked for silk thread, a few members went off to work in a Connecticut mill to learn how to manufacture it. And later when silver spoons sold well, they launched Oneida's most famous product—silverware. But fortune, if not fame, was still a long way off, and the marriage of the group almost went on the rocks. Running a communal household successfully took more than ingenuity, ambition, and faith.

An unlikely product saved the experiment from the fate of most Yankee utopias—extinction. Sewell Newhouse, a former trapper and Indian trader, and one of the first members, had improved the springs on an ordinary steel trap for small animals. The trap sold so well locally that he continued to fill orders after joining the community. When other members began to help him, trap making became a family business. Although it seemed to contradict the Oneida ideal and law of love, Noyes had no scruples about putting everyone to work, including the small children, manufacturing and marketing the deadly Newhouse trap. It developed into the best-selling trap in North America and became the Perfectionists' main support.

Over the years other Oneida enterprises expanded and grew profitable under the guidance of special departments. The community continued to work hard together, with men and women as equals, shielded from worry, and "seeking first the Kingdom of God and its righteousness." They "met with good Providences and answers to prayer when in want of money," relying in part on the spiritual world with which they maintained communication. Outside help became possible for the menial work, and an advanced policy of enlightened working conditions for hirelings was begun. As the long hours of labor were shortened, the "work system" was improved. There was more time for recreation and the continuous education that Noyes considered as important as work.

The big brick steam-heated Mansion House, which replaced the old one in the 1860's, lent itself to the socializing he encouraged. Members were urged to "keep in the circulation." Comfortable rooms and lounges hummed with music and conversation in the evening. Reading rooms and a well-stocked and uncensored library were popular, although excessive novel reading was a weakness liable to family rebuke. In the common dining room adults and children sat around tables that had revolving centers for self-service. The food was plain and did not include tea, coffee, or much meat. Always changing its habits, the community once went on a schedule of only two meals a day. Sometimes the whole household fasted for twenty-four hours.

Every evening from six to eight o'clock a general meet-

ing of the community was held in the Big Hall after dinner.
The men, bearded and solemn, sat with their arms folded, and
the women sewed or knitted in the lamplight at small covered
tables. Each adult had a voice and a vote on matters reported
by the various committees in charge of communal affairs
and business.

When the business meeting was over, Father Noyes, his
red hair and beard turned white, delivered instructive "home
talks." He sat with his eyes closed, wrinkling his forehead and
rubbing his thumb on his vest in a characteristic way, as he
sought inspiration from the Apostle Paul. While a ste-
nographer copied down his words, which were usually published, he discussed Perfectionist theology and its relation to
the primitive church. He would muse aloud about how to
apply it to daily life "for continuing growth and increasing
enjoyment."

"We ought not to make prayer a solemn thing, but go to
work in a fox-hunter's spirit. Start a fox," he challenged, "get
something to pray for—and then make it a lively struggle in
the real spirit of sport. Get your health and education by it,
and learn to know God by it!"

When Noyes was away on one of his frequent trips to
New York or elsewhere, a wide range of events was substi-
tuted for the evening discussion. There were theatricals,
lectures, readings from the outside world's newspapers, musi-
cals, respectable card games, dancing, children's performances
and parties. Sometimes the children sat up in the balcony and
watched their parents doing Virginia reels and quadrilles.

During the day work was varied, and jobs were rotated
to avoid routine. All work was regarded as honorable since it
was for the common good. Laziness was not tolerated. When

prosperity increased, the needs of the members remained simple; everything they required was supplied by the commune. Their life style discouraged greed; no private hoardings or possessions such as jewelry were allowed. At one time, the women were asked to turn over all their brooches and pins as a form of self-denial. The children grew up naturally sharing their playthings.

A lively community newspaper, the Oneida *Circular*,

The Oneida Community library.

kept the outside world posted on the religious beliefs, manner of life, and progress of this perfection-seeking society. Outsiders also came to see Oneida for themselves. Special railroad excursions brought visitors on weekends, when the community held open house. The women's tunic costumes and short hairdos were a big attraction, but, of course, the public was mostly curious about the unusual sexual practices of the members. There were three persistent rumors about their domestic arrangements. The first was that the members distributed themselves by lot at bedtime. A second was that they all slept in one bed, and the third was that the community children did not know who their parents were. To the last rumor the Oneidans had a standard answer: the children, they said, took their word about who their parents were—just as the visitors' children took theirs.

As a matter of fact, the system of complex marriage was very formal. Arrangements and applications for "interviews" were handled by a committee, chaired for years by Noyes and composed of the "central members" who helped him run the community. The system favored the older and more spiritual people, since so-called layers of ascending and descending fellowship played a major role in the entire community life. Members of the family were supposed to seek out their spiritual superiors and be "drawn upward to God" and improved by associating with them.

Noyes had achieved the holiest state; it was understood that he communicated directly with heaven itself. Therefore, he and his close associates, the mature central members, had the duty and privilege of introducing girls and boys to the sacrament of love. The young people could not choose their partners. This decree was usually accepted, since from childhood they were taught "the greater love of God" and the selfishness of "exclusive and idolatrous attachments." Even dolls had been banished from the playroom as a selfish attachment, because little girls made "idols" of them and were distracted from the community spirit. The "doll spirit," Noyes taught, was connected with the worship of images. When dolls were voted out by the community, they were ceremonially burned by the children themselves.

Noyes preached that love was holy and God-given, a sacrament meant to be extended to all who loved God. He pointed with disgust to ordinary marriage, which chained together unmatched natures and caused adultery, divorce, women's diseases, masturbation, and prostitution, not to mention "monotonous and scanty fare" for husband and wife. In sharp contrast to all that, marriage Oneida-style was a continuing courtship that kept the members youthful in spirit, appearance, activity, energy, and outlook.

Even the course of communal love, however, did not always run smoothly. Some Perfectionists suffered from the world's "marriage spirit" instead of the "loving spirit," and were "too claiming and legal." A few hung back from the system altogether. Often, serious "heart affairs" infected the young people, who found it hard to resist their emotions. All such human problems and struggles among the "saints" had to be handled by the strict discipline of mutual criticism.

A member with a problem or defect was summoned to face a committee of critics, or he might offer himself for criticism, sometimes in a public meeting, but more often in private. What he went through was an ordeal, but he usually came out feeling purified and happier. "I was stood on my head until all the self-righteousness drained out of me" was one description of the trial. To another it was like being dissected by a knife. But it was admitted after the soul searching that "all the things they said were true, and they're gone, washed away!"

During an epidemic of diphtheria, which was triumphantly claimed to have been cured by criticism and cracked ice, a patient described his experience: "I was taken at night with a sore throat, which continued to grow worse, and the next day I had all the symptoms of diphtheria. Being no better at night, but rather worse, I sent for a committee. Their criticism immediately threw me into a profuse sweat, till I felt as though I had been in a bath; and before the committee left the room, my headache, backache, and fever were all gone. The criticism had an edge to it, and literally separated me from the spirit of disease that was upon me. . . . I attributed my recovery entirely to the Spirit of truth administered in *criticism*, and believe it to be the best remedy for soul and body. I regret my coldness toward it, and my fear of it in the past."

Noyes was the only one who never submitted to criticism, although he sometimes criticized himself. An uncanny judge of character, he was hard on weak-spirited offenders, particularly the lovesick. He had no sympathy at all for the disease that threatened the communal interest. A young man accused of "exclusive love" would bluntly be advised to be less possessive and to let someone else take his place at the side of the "selfishly adored one." Noyes knew this would not be easy. But then, as he once said, "the true kind of improve-

ment is to do something that requires courage." As a penalty
for partiality, he would order a separation and banish one of
a guilty pair to exile at Wallingford, Connecticut, a branch
community founded in 1850.

When the community children failed to measure up to
perfection, they, too, were subject to sharp criticism, and
sometimes they administered their own. Their sheltered young
lives were as thoroughly regulated and as happy as their
elders'. But they had responsibilities. It was believed that
children should work; the older children, therefore, were
required to make chains for the traps every day after lunch.
They sat on high stools in the large chain room in the base-
ment of the Mansion House, fitting links together and securing
them with a metal twister and a vise worked by a treadle.
Their hands and feet flew for an hour before they were released and sent out to play on the vast community grounds.

Later in the afternoon the children gathered for their own
daily meeting and instruction in Perfectionism. Sometimes
adult members came to read to them from the Bible, or to
tell them stories with a moral. One taught the futility of
selfishness. It was about a man who was so determined to share
none of his belongings that he kept his wife in his pocket. She,
being like-minded, kept her children in her pocket. And the
children kept their playthings in their pockets, so that other
youngsters could not touch them. What good were private
possessions, then, it was made clear to the community children,
if you could not openly enjoy them?

To the Oneida Community it was wrong not to share
loved ones and possessions. The mothers of the community
children struggled not to be selfish. They tried to keep their

Everyone enjoyed the "children's hour."

affection within approved bounds when the children visited them. But communal child rearing was said to be harder on mothers than fathers, and harder on girls than boys. Fathers—those tall distinguished men "with their heads in heaven"—were often quite remote, and none was more distant from his children than John Humphrey Noyes. "I revered him, but he was much too far away, too near to heaven and God," said Pierrepont Burt Noyes, one of Noyes's nine children.

By the time the community could afford children, Noyes was reflecting on the possibility of producing superior progeny. "Every race horse, every straight-backed bull, every premium pig tells us what we can and should do for men," he said. Did not Oneida provide a unique opportunity to restrict mating to those best qualified on physical, mental, moral, and spiritual grounds?

In 1869, before the word "eugenics" was even invented for the science of improving offspring, an experiment at Oneida was under way. Noyes named it "stirpiculture," from the Latin word *stirpes,* meaning stem or stock. Thirty-eight young men, calling themselves "your true soldiers," offered themselves to their leader "to be used in any combinations that may seem to you desirable." They claimed no rights, no privileges, asking "only to be servants of the truth." Fifty-three young women also declared:

1. That we do not belong to *ourselves* in any respect, that we *do* belong first to *God* and second to Mr. Noyes as God's true representative.
2. That we have no rights or personal feelings in regard to child-bearing which shall in the least degree oppose or embarrass him in his choice of scientific combination.
3. That we will put aside all envy, childishness and self-seeking, and rejoice with those who are chosen candidates; that we will, if necessary, become martyrs to science, and cheerfully resign all desires to become mothers if for any reason Mr. Noyes deems us unfit material. Above all, we offer ourselves as "living sacrifices" to God and true Communism.

It was up to Noyes and a committee of central members to decide which applications to accept and who should mate with whom. Naturally, he could find no one more eligible than himself. Therefore Noyes—already in his sixties —participated along with 100 others. Eighty-one became parents. The fathers, on the average twelve years older than the mothers, were considered more important in determining the quality of the offspring. Fifty-eight stirpicultural babies, four of them stillborn, came into the world. Although they were not singled out for special attention, the "stirpicults" were studied from infancy with special interest as they went through the progressive community school and often on to college to study medicine, science, mechanics, or the arts.

It had always been a policy of the community to send good students away for higher education. Leaving home was considered a broadening experience for those who had grown up forbidden to speak to outsiders, even to the hired help. But, away from home, they felt for the first time their difference from others and the peculiarities of their parents. At a distance the Oneida community looked less respectable. Its reputation was terrible, and the "good people" back there seemed like religious fanatics!

The students began to question Perfectionism. Philosophy and science courses led to uncertainty about the very existence of God, let alone the special status of John Humphrey Noyes as a divine agent.

Brought up to avoid any friendship that excluded others, some young people discovered that they preferred separate love, and a private life with a single partner and one's own children. They went home in the 1870's full of discontents and doubts. It further disturbed them to learn that Father Noyes wanted to retire and proposed to turn over the community leadership to his only legitimate son, Dr. Theodore Noyes, born in the Putney days. But the community objected to the Yale-educated doctor. He was no longer a practicing Perfectionist but a freethinker. He had inherited none of his father's personal magnetism or gift for leadership. And, besides, he did not particularly want the job.

By 1877, however, the elder Noyes, by now quite deaf and growing weak in voice, was ineffective and unable to participate in the important daily meeting. The central members functioned in his stead until, in 1877, Father Noyes appointed a governing committee and installed Theodore as its head. For a year or so Theodore served the community, exerting most of his influence on the stirpiculture committee, where he looked for the best physical, rather than spiritual, qualities in prospective parents. At one point, however, he left the community. The rest of the governing committee, fending for itself, faced internal dissension. The membership split into two parties: those who remained loyal to John Noyes and those who objected to his despotic, one-man rule. Under a man named Towner, who had joined the community only in 1874, Noyes's right to be "first husband" and to initiate young girls into complex marriage was contested. Those who supported the community's founding father called it God's will, since Noyes represented heaven's interest on earth. The real issue was his continuing right to leadership, which the opposing party wanted to be more democratic. The division was deep and reflected the loss of faith in the religious ideals that justified Oneida's way of life and never allowed it to be questioned. Over the years business expansion had come to overshadow spiritual growth, even though Noyes had warned, "If we have primarily in view to make money, we shall get no enthusiasm from heaven, for we shift from our true purpose."

While the two parties clashed and threatened to shatter the vision of Perfection, Oneida's arch enemy was adding pressure from without. He was John W. Mears, a professor at nearby Hamilton College. In 1873 this angry neighbor had begun a savage crusade to destroy the Oneida Community. Upstate and down he revealed its sexual practices, accused its sinners of rape and adultery, and demanded an end to its "immoralities." Now Mears joined forces with New York clergymen in a determined effort to end Oneida.

By June, 1879, their attacks had grown fierce. There was no strong opposition from the divided community; in fact, there was a suspicion of some complicity. The threat of arrest was so real that Noyes reacted in the same way he had done once before. In the still of a summer night he suddenly left Oneida, just as he had fled from Vermont thirty-two years before, and found safety over the Canadian border. This time, he refrained from defending his notorious family against an angry public. Instead he startled the Oneida members by agreeing with Theodore, who was back on the new administrative council, that they should give up the most controversial custom, complex marriage. He sent a message begging the community to show that Christian communism could survive without it. But Oneida had lost too much. It no longer had divinely inspired leadership or a united faith in Perfectionism. And when the members voted to abandon complex marriage, it lost the basis of its social system.

Thirty-seven conventional unions took place "to protect the children." Many of the adults had joined the community as married couples and resumed that status. But there were many children left over whom the world would regard as bastards, and there were sixteen unmarried women under forty who would be branded because they had lived by what they were taught to regard as most holy.

"Don't worry," the assorted mothers of John Noyes's children tried to comfort them, "we consider you children more legitimate than any in the world!" But some of the women needed comforting themselves since Noyes could not marry any of them. His loyal, legal wife Harriet was at his side in Canada.

In the Oneida Community private marriage at once caused the competition and possessiveness that Noyes had tried to abolish by substituting an unselfish system. True communalism as he envisioned it came to an end, although a dignified one. Instead of abolishing the community and selling its properties, it was agreed to "divide and reorganize" in the form of a joint-stock company that would continue to operate the community industries. There would then be jobs and dividends, and no one would be cast out into the world. In 1880 the old community was reborn as the Oneida Community, Limited. It took charge of the community's businesses —silverware, chains, traps, silk thread, and canning. Shares in the new company were divided among the 226 members, based on their original contribution and length of service in the community. Some kept their shares while others sold them. Many ex-members stayed on in the Mansion House, paying for room and board, or moved to separate houses nearby.

Those who worked for the company received wages for the first time. A few former members moved away, requesting that their dividends be mailed in plain envelopes to avoid embarrassment and prejudice.

Those who remained at Oneida tried to adjust to the new system and even to preserve a communal way of life. It was a novel experience for them to take any private action, manage money, or own anything, and they were scrupulous about returning even a borrowed pin. Divisions continued among them, however, and there was a trend away from religion altogether. As Perfectionism waned, revivalist meetings were held in an attempt to strengthen it; even spiritualism was introduced and grew influential. When Towner and his followers realized that they could never hope to gain control of the community and the new company, he led an exodus of the major rebels against John Noyes to California. This left the loyalists in control of the company. The new directors had Noyes's approval, and he had the satisfaction once again of feeling that he was the true leader.

At seventy he was still an optimist, boasting that the Oneida Community was planned by the heavenly powers and had a wonderful future. With a faithful few he lived several years longer in the stone cottage that the community provided for him on the Canadian side of the Niagara Falls, where he continued to preach to his reduced household against the worldly spirit. His own faith never wavered. He never doubted his role as an agent of heaven who was destined to establish a holy community on earth in the wake of the Second Coming of Jesus Christ.

Noyes spent his last years in Bible study and contempla-

OUT OF THE FOLD.

"Oh, dreadful! They dwell in peace and harmony, and have no church scandals. They must be wiped out."

tion, sometimes sharing theological insights with the loyal Perfectionists who had left Oneida to join him. His children came to visit him, as did some ex-members who worked in the spoon and chain-manufacturing businesses that the company had moved to the American side of Niagara Falls for the economic advantage of the water power. Noyes sent encouragement, spiritual advice, and even direct-mail criticisms to Oneida. But he never returned. He died in Canada in 1886 at the age of seventy-five. The community at Oneida received his body and buried it simply. It was never its custom—or his —to grieve for the departed with "long doleful faces."

His wife went back to her old home, where she survived her husband by ten years. She and the other aging members resigned themselves to the new order. And the young ex-members, reared in isolation and innocence, ventured out into the world, where many were successful in business careers, diplomacy, and the arts. Pierrepont Burt Noyes, one of the most gifted of the generation of "stirpiculunts," later returned to the fold to restore some of the lofty spirit of his father's utopian communism to the floundering but promising capitalist company.

Descendants of the "Honorable John" and the famous nonconformers of Oneida still live upstate in or near the stately Mansion House on its green lawn. Many wings of the big house have been divided into apartments. There still seems to linger around the mansion a whisper of the old nineteenth-century gossip about those who rest together in the cemetery. Proud of and amused at their ancestors' daring, today's Oneida families remain comfortable and proper in a multimillion-dollar silver and stainless steel tableware business noted for its industrial idealism.

Brides selecting Oneida Community patterns rarely know that there was a real Oneida Community, where every member was the bride or groom of every other. Americans, who respect success in business, coexisted with this far-out Yankee commune for thirty years before demanding its breakup. And that gave the Oneida Community a chance to develop spiritual, social, intellectual, scientific, industrial, and psychological insights that are still revolutionary today.

CHAPTER V

The Society of Brothers

LOVE AND MARRIAGE

And He prophesied and foretold a kingdom,
a rule of God which was to change
completely the conditions and the
order of the world and make them new.
To acknowledge this, to live according to this—I believe
is God's command for this hour.

—Eberhard Arnold, 1920

Eberhard Arnold lay helpless on a sofa, his leg in a cast, while the Gestapo searched the farmhouse. No one was allowed to leave the room, and every door was guarded as all books, papers, and letters—especially from outside Germany —were examined for information hostile to the state. The Nazis had grown suspicious of the small farm community called the Rhön Bruderhof which refused to say "Heil Hitler." Something subversive to the Fatherland must be going on. Why was there such coming and going at Herr Arnold's "place of the brothers" in central Germany, where families claimed to be living according to Jesus' Sermon on the Mount?

Late that evening the Gestapo drove off in a police car loaded with books and manuscripts. From then on the communal farm was closely watched. No more guests were allowed, no novices admitted to learn the one true way of life that could make the world new. The schoolchildren—the community's own and those it took in and brought up as its own—were tested to see if they were patriotically instructed. When they could not sing the Hitler songs, the community was assigned a Nazi teacher.

But when the teacher showed up, there were no pupils. A vacation in Switzerland had been hurriedly arranged for the children, who never returned to Germany. Next, the teenagers came under suspicion for failing to join Hitler Youth when it marched triumphantly through the villages and the Bruderhof itself. Finally, the young men of draft age were suspected of trying to dodge military service on the grounds of the community's pacifist convictions.

One by one, the younger people disappeared from the commune, sent by foot, rail, and bicycle to Liechtenstein, the tiny principality between Switzerland and Austria. There, in an unused hotel high in the snow-covered Alps, they were joined by the children and their teachers, who could no longer stay in the Swiss school where they had taken refuge.

It grew very quiet in the Rhön Bruderhof, where Eberhard Arnold was suffering from complications following surgery on his leg. The community had no income and no prospects. State support was withdrawn for the school and for the poor and wandering, who had always been welcome there. The publication of inspirational books was forbidden. All hope focused on the new commune, the Alm Bruderhof in Liechtenstein, and trips were made to Holland and England to raise funds to support it and to look for a better location.

After a second operation Arnold's leg had to be amputated, and in 1935 he died. During his final delirium, in a hospital full of Nazis, he had shouted a dangerous question: "Have Hitler and Goebbels repented?" It was a futile hope. Nazism grew in power, and the Gestapo kept its eye on the small defiant commune that had lost its leader. The death of Eberhard Arnold at the age of fifty-two shocked those who had gathered around him, but it did not destroy their spirit or their determination to go on.

Eberhard Arnold was born in 1883 in Königsberg, East Prussia, where his father, born in Williamsfield, Ohio, was a schoolteacher. It was an uncle, a minister, and not his parents, who planted in the boy the dream of Christian brotherhood as the only hope of the world.

As a child Arnold worried his parents by making friends with poor people and bringing home tramps. Once they discovered lice on him after he had exchanged hats with one of them. When he was sixteen, they sent him to spend a vacation with his uncle. Working in his uncle's parish among the underpaid weavers, and later with the Salvation Army, Arnold was impressed by people who tried to put Christianity into practice. A strong conversion experience brought him closer to God than to the organized church, and for years he tried to bring others to Jesus.

Writing and editing religious newspapers and books, serving as an official in the German Student Christian Movement, Arnold boldly denounced the church and the state for tolerating social injustice and greed. More and more he was drawn to the poverty and the path of the primitive church. He found the perfect helpmate in Emmy von Hollander, whom he married "in the Spirit" in 1909. Together they continued to seek a better way to serve man and God than purely personal

Eberhard Arnold, founder, with his wife, of the Bruderhof communal movement in Germany, which became the Society of Brothers in the United States in 1954.

religion. Reading the old scriptures and ancient religious writings, they discovered the same longing among the Anabaptists of the sixteenth century. Thousands of these peaceful people in Switzerland and the Tyrol had given up private property and middle-class existence to live a communal religious life.

In open-house meetings in Berlin where they lived, at

Emmy Arnold married Eberhard in 1909. She survives her husband and today lives in the community at Rifton, New York.

town and country conferences, and in lecture halls where Arnold declared his views, the couple was surrounded by troubled members of the youth movement, wanting direction and sensing the need for a new morality among the German people. World War I intensified their despair as the nation was crushed and defeated. Arnold wrote of witnessing unbeliev-able suffering and shocking sights during those years—the carting of children's bodies, wrapped only in newspaper, through the city to mass burials; desperate people—reduced to a diet of turnips—rushing to cut meat from a starved horse that dropped dead in the street; disabled young soldiers unable to return to the arms of their wives. At the same time there was widespread corruption and unjust privilege among well-to-do "Christian" families. To Eberhard Arnold this was not the Christianity of Jesus or the way of the Sermon on the Mount.

In 1920 Arnold gave up his job, and he and Emmy bought the farm at Sannerz. They and their five children opened their hearts and home to all who wanted to join them in being true Christians, sharing everything in the unselfish manner of the primitive church.

The young had arrived in droves at Sannerz—more than a thousand the first year—making it necessary to move to a larger farm, the Rhön Bruderhof. There the families and many guests united in the farm work, gardening, handcrafts, caring for and teaching the children, and publishing tracts in a small print shop. No one was turned away, and everyone received encouragement and help. So faithful was the united household to the teachings of Jesus that once two strong members allowed themselves to be robbed while walking through the woods with the wages of the family workers in their pocket.

Fifteen years later, in 1935, with a second World War threatening, it was once more the young people—this time in exile—who kept the spirit of communal brotherhood alive in country after country.

In Liechtenstein, where the young Bruderhof men of military age had fled from German fascism, the officials were now afraid to keep the draft resisters. Forced to leave, the brothers formed a troupe of strolling players, and with lutes, guitars, and flutes they worked their way across the Alps and through France. They crossed the borders at night, miraculously escaping the notice of customs officials. They were in danger of disappearing into concentration camps for not having passports, which the German consulate in Liechtenstein had not renewed when they refused to salute and say "Heil Hitler." The troupe finally reached England and found generous friends there to help build a new Bruderhof community.

Meanwhile, the Rhön Bruderhof continued in poverty and daily suspense. Suddenly in 1937, without warning, it was pronounced "not desired in Germany" and ordered by the Gestapo to be dissolved within twenty-four hours.

Visiting the community at that time were two "relatives" from America, dark-suited brethren from the ancient Hutterite church-communities whose founder, Jakob Hutter, had been burned at the stake in 1536. Eberhard Arnold felt a spiritual kinship with them. In 1930 he had traveled to the American Northwest and Canada to visit the Hutterites on their prosperous mechanized farms. He formed a link between the new Bruderhof and these descendants of an Anabaptist communistic and pacifist sect founded during the Reformation in South Germany and the Tyrol. For 400 years the Hutterites had lived in strict isolation, allowing no intermarriage even when religious persecution in the sixteenth century drove them to other countries. In the 1870's, faced with military conscription, 300 members migrated from southern Russia to

South Dakota, with some financial help from the German-American religious community of George Rapp.

There Arnold found them isolating themselves in the same way their forefathers had lived in Moravia in the sixteenth century, with "full community of goods, communal work and worship, and a common table." Even their costume had barely changed, and the men used hooks and eyes on their coats and vests in accordance with an old custom. The Hutterite brothers received Arnold into membership, with the "laying on of hands," and confirmed him in the ministry of the Word. After a year-long visit, he returned to Germany.

To mark their affiliation in 1931 with this antique communal sect, the Bruderhof gave up with regret its beloved music and songs and took down the pictures from the walls. "Let us sing and play to God in our hearts," their new kinsmen instructed. The sisters of the Bruderhof began wearing head scarves and peasant dresses, which they did not mind, although no one liked the dark drab suits adopted by the men. Smoking was also abandoned. In return for this sacrifice they derived "roots" and community of spirit, if not the financial help they could have used at the time.

The two visiting Hutterite elders were shocked when they witnessed the Nazi seizure of communal Bruderhof property and buildings in 1937. "You're worse than the Americans!" they cried. They told the Nazis how the Americans during World War I had given them protection when they had to emigrate to Canada because of their refusal to fight. "Why can't you treat this community so?" they demanded. In answer the Nazis stole their traveling money and herded them into one room with their hosts. There they all went hungry until the police carried out everything they wanted from the farmhouse and left.

It was raining when the hour arrived for the members to leave their home. When the sun suddenly shone on their exodus, it seemed an answer to their prayers for help. With the little they owned on their backs and with the sick and old and a newborn baby among them, they paused at the grave of Eberhard Arnold and went into exile.

Left behind with the unmade beds and dirty dishes from the interrupted meals, with the communal laundry still soaking in the washtubs, the two Hutterite elders recorded in their diaries, "It seemed we'd come to Europe to be reminded of what it means to be driven from one's house and home. God has protected us in America from such misery. Our migration to Canada, when we had to sell everything we had, was nothing like this."

The refugees made their way to England, where all were reunited at a new farm community in the Cotswolds. In those darkening days, many Englishmen joined them to work for peace and brotherhood at the Cotswold Bruderhof in Ashton Keynes, Wiltshire, and at a second branch called Oaksey. Later many chose to emigrate with the German members, who were considered enemy aliens during World War II and had to leave England or be interned for the duration.

But where in the world could they all go? The United States did not want a German pacifist group that would not bear arms in wartime. And, anyway, because they married, the celibate Shakers in America refused to sell them property sought by an agent on their behalf. Only the poor little

country of Paraguay opened its doors to the German-English group.

It was a long hard peonage in the semitropical wilderness of South America for those used to North European climates. But, thankful to be together, the Primavera ("spring" in Spanish) Bruderhof managed to farm the land and raise cattle. They developed three small villages and opened a hos-

The Woodcrest Community at Rifton, New York, first North American branch of the Society of Brothers.

pital for natives. To get help for the hospital, the brothers journeyed north, to the United States, where they made friends with Quakers and visited other communes. Through these new friends, some of whom went back with them to live the communal life in Paraguay, the first postwar move to the United States was made possible.

In July, 1954, the brothers came to rest on a hilltop

property called Woodcrest at Rifton, New York, not far from Kingston. A long roundabout way had led to this land of greater promise. The name Bruderhof was changed to the Society of Brothers, although the old name persisted. And the brothers set about proving wrong the Shaker eldress who rejected their system, saying, "True communal living cannot be realized on the basis of the private family."

The old Yankee communes often went to the extremes of celibacy or group marriage, but this new one preserved the natural family. Its families with their many children moved into small apartments in the assorted houses on the ninety-five-acre former estate sprawling over a hillside. The main residence, a white Victorian mansion, became a schoolhouse, in which classes began almost immediately. The community whose children are all-important found the perfect means of support in the manufacture of wooden educational toys. They called them "Community Playthings."

When the toy business was well-established, a second commune was founded at Farmington, Pennsylvania, and a third at Norfolk, Connecticut. By 1966 all members remaining in Paraguay and most of those still working together in a castle near London were gathered into the American colonies. Many Americans joined them to work for the peace and brotherhood that Eberhard Arnold preached while the Nazi secret police prowled outside the door.

Today each rural commune holds all things common in imitation of the early Christians, sharing what one brother calls "a life of joy and service, richer with marriage and children." No longer affiliated with the Hutterites, there are now 800 members, still aglow with the vision of a man who died thirty-five years ago and who has never been replaced as leader. His disciples continue to protest a warring, intolerant, and to them intolerable, world in a full-time demonstration of the good life men could lead if everyone loved his neighbor as much as himself. Their social action is at home—in the social gospel of Jesus. The living looks easy at the community in Rifton, and the place like a mountain resort or work camp. Friendly, casually dressed men who never wear ties, women who never wear make-up, and rosy unspoiled children go brightly about their common work and schooling. But each day demands renewal on their part of the fanatic faith that builds lasting Yankee utopias.

Visitors are surprised that there is no house of worship in the church-community at the end of a long driveway winding past the toy factory and up a wooded hill. At the crest, where a spire might be expected to rise, is the schoolhouse, and clustered around it are houses named to honor the past, such as Sannerz, the first Bruderhof, and Primavera, the jungle home. Ranged around a big central lawn are workshops, a sewing and mending room, and a laundry. Nearby is the Baby House or day-care center for the youngest brothers and sisters.

A plain two-story building that looks like a social hall—and is—has replaced an ornamental old carriage house that burned down. This is the heart of the community; it contains offices, a library and reading rooms, as well as a large comfortable kitchen and the huge dining room where members take two meals together almost every day. Twice a week there are family suppers at home. The bright blue sunlit room is feast hall, conference room, meetinghouse and chapel.

Decked with flowers and murals and bowers from past wed-
dings and celebrations, it features an old wooden beam
transported from the Rhön Bruderhof, from which the first
brothers were expelled. In the wood, carved in German, is
the credo of the Society of Brothers:

> That we from our hearts
> Love one another,
> Of one mind
> In peace remain together.

The words can be contemplated during the silence that
begins each common meal before a brief song breaks the
silence. At noon families sit together around long tables,
the unmarried members among them. Present among the
Arnolds is Emmy Arnold, 86, the white-haired widow of
Eberhard, who with her children helped found the first
Bruderhof community. It is half a century since she came
to believe with him that to be a Christian meant living the
way taught by Jesus in the Sermon on the Mount. Still well
and active, she is devoted to the community that includes
her own sixty-odd grandchildren and great-grandchildren.

About half of the 300 people gathered at Rifton are
under fifteen. The older elementary-school children lunch
with the adults, while the younger ones eat and nap in their
schoolrooms. Babies from six weeks to three years spend the
day in the nursery in the care of mothers; high-school students
attend public school in Kingston.

At lunch the children are entertained by a chapter from
a book, read aloud as bowls of macaroni salad and platters
of cold cuts are passed around each table. Bowls for second

helpings are held up for the *austeilers*—the German word for the boys and men who work as waiters—to refill in the kitchen. The week's cooks and bakers are provided with staples by the community steward, and vegetables, fresh and home-canned, come from the children's garden, the communal cupboard, and government surplus.

The simple, almost spare meal ends with a second period of silence before everyone quietly leaves, first handing the dishes to one end of the table. In the lobby some linger at the bulletin board or check the list of assignments for the week's *austeilers*, dishwashers, cleaning teams, and baby watchers to relieve mothers for evening meetings and meals.

Most people go straight home to relax with the children. The men return to work at two in the office, school, book bindery, and the small factory where the playthings are built and shipped out. The women—who teach, work in the office, write and illustrate books, and rotate jobs in the kitchen, laundry, sewing room, and storeroom—stay home with the children until three. The younger children come home to join them; then everyone goes back to school or work until five o'clock.

In late afternoon the public-school bus drops off the "high-schoolers" at the foot of the driveway. They usually head for the kitchen to have a snack and a chance to talk over the events of the day with their special adult counselors. This junior brotherhood, not yet members and no longer sheltered from the conflicting ways of the world, sometimes has problems.

By day they move among teen-agers wearing mini-skirts, heavy make-up, and the hippie outfits of a typical city high school. Their own old-fashioned clothes and the girls' braids and pigtails stand out as "different." The innocence they reflect baffles their classmates, who find their life apart strange. A few fellow students become interested in it, however, and become good friends; one girl sang in the choir at a Woodcrest wedding. The community scholars are serious about their studies. They do not date and have little time for extracurricular activities at school. So much goes on at home, where they are occupied with meetings, music groups, plays, festivals, folk dancing, hikes, and special outings. Besides, they all have jobs and responsibilities.

Folk dancing is part of community life.

After high school, young people are often sent away to colleges that the community can afford, or to technical schools, as much for education in life as for further training. If they choose to remain in the community, as many do after some experience of the world outside, they serve the same long apprenticeship as any novice. No one inherits membership in the Society of Brothers; there is no infant baptism. That ceremony takes place when an adult receives membership, if that is his or her choice. Membership is a serious step and a total lifetime commitment.

So is marriage. For this reason, frank discussion in their college classes of divorce and infidelity sometimes upsets students from the community, who have been known to walk out rather than listen. Professors are unlikely to know many young people today who regard marriage as permanent and sex as sacred in uniting man and woman in love and service of God.

It is not expected that everyone can accept the brothers' marriage requirement, fulfill its vows, or agree with its view of the husband as the "head" of the wife, except those who marry "in the spirit." Therefore, marriages take place only within the community, where "two become one in Christ." No outsider can be brought in; a member must withdraw from the community to marry one.

A wedding is a long happy celebration, involving young and old. Months ahead, furniture and gifts are made, rooms painted and readied, special songs composed, and decorations planned. Somehow, surprises are kept secret until the day the holy ceremony takes place. The bride wears the favorite adornment of the young—a garland of fresh flowers in her hair and a simple white handmade dress. The groom wears an open-necked white shirt, and there are no ties, formal suits, or high heels among the wedding guests. After the ceremony they all trail the couple across the grass to the marriage feast. Later the men perform morris dances, introduced by the English members, and the children dance and sing.

Wedding sentiment lasts. When newlyweds who have moved to a branch community come home or visit, they are welcomed by a special candlelit meal. The extended family expresses its unity and love in breaking bread together and in song, which is as much a part of its life as music was to the Rappites.

Singing is still as characteristic of the group as it was of the early Bruderhof, which sacrificed music for kinship with the Hutterites. Long since restored, not only at meals, but at business and religious meetings of the brotherhood, song has a place on the agenda and in the order of service, and seals each unanimous decision or family prayer. At Rifton there are four choirs as well as one community and two school orchestras.

The sound of music at seven o'clock in the morning, however, is more likely to be the family radio. After breakfast at home the children leave at eight for school, and the men go to work. Mothers have an extra hour to do the breakfast dishes and tidy the house. Their housework is light, since the halls and bathrooms shared by two families are cleaned by different teams every week. The family laundry is washed and dried in the communal laundry once a week, with daily service for babies.

Mending is taken care of in the sewing room, where a

large supply of hand-me-downs get new zippers and patches. Most of the women's longish, dirndl skirts and blouses are made from community patterns, but the women and girls do not dress alike. The communal household is well organized: each season the group housemothers ask the women what new clothing they need for their families and what old clothing needs repair. The housemothers also receive special family requests for birthdays, a time when a man who appreciates a bottle of brandy gets it, or a girl is given an embroidered skirt.

Each household reflects the different backgrounds and cultures of the members. There are now more American and English members than German, in addition to Swiss, Belgians, and Canadians. Far from being monastic and barren, their apartments are full of plants, books, pictures, and souvenirs of the past. Some elaborate cages have been installed for the children's birds, and hutches have been built for the popular small pets like hamsters, guinea pigs, and even chinchilla. There are few cats and dogs because experience has proved them to be poor communitarians. Too aggressive and not prone to sharing affection or anything else, the dog and cat population is being allowed to die out.

The first great community pet was a donkey named Eeyore. The only loner for years in the commune, he lived in a field beyond the schoolhouse in a stable built by the children. It took three men to work him, and later Eeyore was succeeded by a pair of ponies. Every day there are excursions from the Baby House to feed bruised apples and tidbits to the animals.

There is a story that a three-year-old toddling to the

ponies spied a group of visiting teachers. The women wore hats, under which their faces were powdered and painted. Certainly they did not look like his mothers and sisters and baby-tenders, who wear no cosmetics. With glee he pointed at them and shouted, "Clownies!" He had decided they were from the circus.

While pets and community playthings keep the babies happy, the older children are inspired by treasured folkways of the members and by the holiday seasons. Christmas and Easter are given true observance, while the highlight of fall is a symbolic lantern festival, an old German tradition prepared for weeks ahead. At the noon and evening meals there are old and new songs about lanterns. In the evening parents and children gather in the schoolrooms to make the strong paper lanterns they carry by wire handles, with candles inside, on the night the lantern parade takes place. The entire community celebrates with the children the spiritual light that the lanterns give the world, the light that streams down from their "city on a hill." "Let your light so shine before men," said Jesus in his Sermon on the Mount, "that they may see your good works and give glory to your Father, who is in heaven."

If it rains and the parade is called off and postponed, the children are greatly disappointed. But someone comes to surprise them. The youngsters lean out the windows as lighted lanterns move in the dark toward their houses. The young adult group, known by the Hebrew name of Shalomers, make the rounds of the families, singing lantern songs and bringing huge trays of homemade doughnuts.

This love of children and desire to enlighten the world

Three-year-olds take a trip across community grounds. Eberhard
Arnold said that "every child is an idea of God."

and share their spiritual heritage with it led the brothers into
a second industrial enterprise, the Plough Publishing House. In
1964 a small printing press was set up at the Farmington
community and a bindery at Rifton. There the inspired
writings of Eberhard Arnold, Christoph Blumhardt, and
other religious leaders, some unknown to the American
public, were handset and printed. Emmy Arnold set down
moving recollections of the early struggle of the Bruderhof
communities. And a special series of juvenile song- and story-

books was developed. Hand-lettered music and poems and old-fashioned sentimental illustrations make them unique in the mass production of children's books.

The same kind of loving, Shakerlike craftsmanship goes into the personalized manufacture of toys in three factories, one at each community. Most of the men share in the creation of the large, uncomplicated, long-lasting wooden playthings, play equipment, and small-scale furniture. Designs grow from the experience and needs of their own communally raised children, and naturally include no war toys. Popular with nursery groups, boards of education, and church schools, the toys encourage children to play together and not alone, and to learn, as one must in community, to co-operate.

To the small quiet business office come orders and payments from all over the world. Trucks owned jointly by the three communes travel back and forth among them, carrying raw materials and finished playthings. The tiny country post office at the hamlet of Rifton is kept busy as sales of more than a million dollars a year underwrite brotherhood and the common life.

Instead of expanding the business, the joint owners choose to continue the present rate of production. Making toys is not the basis of their way of life but only a means to it. And it keeps the members in a far more comfortable style of life, for all its simplicity, than during the first days of poverty remembered by Emmy Arnold. With less struggle to survive and a good measure of success, there is now danger in security itself. Some members who have known persecution fear complacency.

"We don't like to be called a utopia," says Johann

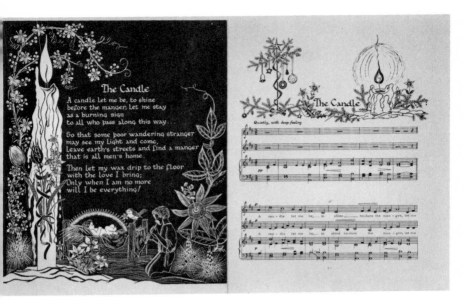

Words and music of a Christmas song framed in pictures, from a book published by the community.

Christoph Arnold, a tall, rangy grandson of Eberhard, with an engaging German manner of expression. The task assigned to him by the community is handling the sale of books, and Christoph goes tieless and relaxed to publishers' hard-selling conventions with a big black iron plough as a trademark. To him, utopia implies a life of ease and selfish luxury, the end of struggle and a goal already reached.

But the living only *looks* easy in the church-community in the mountains; it demands great personal effort. "We're not a community of saints," explains Christoph, "but humans with human problems. We have to struggle and work to cure them. We want to live together as brothers and to show such a life in peace and brotherhood is possible. But we have to seek again and again the strong spirit we had in the beginning."

Each novice spends a long trial period—a time of testing —living the daily life of the community before he dedicates his life, harder to relinquish than his property, to the brotherhood. He ends all outside associations, contributes his worldly goods, and makes certain fundamental promises. After adult baptism ends his novitiate, he surrenders to a life for others that permits no backsliding, no compromise; he no longer "belongs to himself." He accepts the attempt of his brothers and sisters to improve him; if he is not "loving" enough, someone first speaks to him privately. If his fault continues, the whole community—"united in deepest openness"—tries to help and find out why. In a system reminiscent of Oneida's mutual criticism, he takes plain speaking from the group.

One young woman, born in an English Bruderhof, explains: "We have weaknesses in trying to live the way we want to, and it's easier together. We gain strength from each other."

Membership offers more than group therapy. It provides for all basic wants and needs. No one has money, except the allowance that students get for high school. No one has his own car, but all share ten, plus a school bus for outings on Sunday afternoon or trips to take the children to city libraries. No one has insurance; everyone is sure of being cared for when ill or hospitalized. When a member dies, he has a simple funeral. For one evening the body reposes in a homemade coffin, attended by two brothers, while the community pays its respects. Burial takes place the next day in the communal burial ground, and that night a "love feast" is held in the member's memory, and his life and character are recalled.

Leaders naturally come to the fore, not as "human leaders," but "merely to put into action that which is felt by all." No one follows the leader; it is he who follows. In closed meetings the adult members debate their course of action until all are of one mind and there is no ill will; every

A meeting of the brotherhood. Debate at meetings goes on until all are of one mind.

decision is unanimous. They choose spiritual guides, or Servants of the Word—an ancient title for those responsible for the "inner life" of the community—to conduct religious meetings on Sunday evenings, to which outsiders are never admitted. The brotherhood also appoints the foremen of the factory, a steward of the common purse, and women to serve as housemothers. Those who hold such posts are responsible to everyone and keep the members informed of all details of business and budget and the state of the large, well-stocked, and very orderly storeroom, as well as distribution of supplies.

The Society of Brothers considers such fellowship in the service of God and the way of Jesus a better road to a new world than either politics or revolution. The members do not vote in national or local elections or salute the American flag. No Fatherland comes before conscience and God. But they pay taxes and respect the laws that guarantee tolerance for their dissent and opportunity for their expansion.

Unlike the Hutterites, who are probably the largest communal but uncommunicative group in America, the brothers do not cut themselves off from the world and its suffering. The evening meal is often followed by a long news roundup, which reports the prospects for peace and the many problems of the day. Some brothers marched for civil rights, and delegations have protested the war in Vietnam. The young men register their conscientious objection with the local draft board.

Although many young Americans also seek peace on earth and feel the same bond of love, and the same need for close companionship instead of solitary competition, they do not enter the Society of Brothers. Many visit the holy communes, where they are welcome as long as they work. They are as charmed by the idea of living in community as Robert Owen was in the 1820's, when he visited the Shakers before founding his own utopia. But few have enough courage and conviction to stay. Nor have black people responded to this radical religious calling despite its true equality.

The separatists who do join are devout people like the Shakers and the Rappites and the Perfectionists, who expect the world to be better. Like them, they dedicate themselves to the future world promised long ago to the first Christians.

They include former ministers, lawyers, writers, musicians, artists, skilled industrial workers, C.O.'s of other wars, Quakers, idealists, and reformers once interested in consumer co-operatives and communes that tried to revive poor areas in the South. Some once organized communities of their own. Some are Jewish refugees from Hitler's Germany. Many well-educated Americans, disillusioned with "a system of heartlessness and war," find their way to the alternative held out by the Society of Brothers.

To Eberhard Arnold it was no alternative. It was the only practical way for men to live. He came to this conclusion after years of compassion for the poor and concern for men's souls. He realized that Jesus himself must have been interested in more than souls when he made the blind see, the lame walk, and the deaf hear, and that he had prescribed a practical way for men to *live* in his Sermon on the Mount. The Society of Brothers is based on returning to that way of total love, which abolishes selfish rights and privilege and says, "If you have two coats, give one to him who has none. Give food to the hungry. When you are asked for an hour's work, give two. If you want to found a family, then see that all others who want to found a family are able to do so. If you wish education, work, and satisfying activity, make these possible for other people also."

Small bands of people living this way for others, said Eberhard Arnold, will some day merge into one, with a single goal ". . . in a kingdom, a rule of God . . . to change completely the conditions and the order of the world and make them new. To live according to this I believe is God's command for this hour."

And so the Society of Brothers lives, a small, slowly growing band of believers, offering brotherhood to those strong enough to accept. No remnant or relative of any group of the past, this is a great Yankee commune of the present. It is as certain of the new order coming, and as inspirational to a new communal movement as the old sects that pioneered in the American way of utopian community.

There is still a small number—very small it may be, but I think it increases—to whom the old ways, the old purposes of life have become impossible of pursuit—who must breathe freely or be stifled—who cannot live longer to merely personal ends—who will readily dig ditches, if that be the most useful employment which solicits them, but who must do even this heroically, not sordidly, or not at all. They are ready to welcome drudgery, privation, obscurity, but not willing that the covering and cherishing of their own bodies shall be the purpose of their life-long struggle.

—Horace Greeley (1811–1872)